D0421646

Social Work and Foster Care

Social Work and Foster Care

HELEN COSIS BROWN

Series Editor: Keith Brown

BMC

Belfast Metropolitan College

Millfield LRC

Los Angeles | London | New Delhi
Singapore | Washington DC

Learning Matters
An imprint of SAGE Publications Ltd
1 Oliver's Yard
55 City Road
London EC1Y 1SP

SAGE Publications Inc.
2455 Teller Road
Thousand Oaks, California 91320

SAGE Publications India Pvt Ltd
B 1/I 1 Mohan Cooperative Industrial Area
Mathura Road
New Delhi 110 044

SAGE Publications Asia-Pacific Pte Ltd
3 Church Street
#10–04 Samsung Hub
Singapore 049483

Editor: Luke Block
Development editor: Lauren Simpson
Production controller: Chris Marke
Project management: Swales & Willis Ltd, Exeter, Devon
Marketing manager: Tamara Navaratnam
Cover design: Wendy Scott
Typeset by: C&M Digitals (P) Ltd, Chennai, India
Printed by Henry Ling Limited at The Dorset Press, Dorchester, DT1 1HD

© Helen Cosis Brown 2014

First published 2014

Apart from any fair dealing for the purposes of research or private study, or criticism or review, as permitted under the Copyright, Design and Patents Act, 1988, this publication may be reproduced, stored or transmitted in any form, or by any means, only with the prior permission in writing of the publishers, or in the case of reprographic reproduction, in accordance with the terms of licences issued by the Copyright Licensing Agency. Enquiries concerning reproduction outside these terms should be sent to the publishers.

Library of Congress Control Number: 2013954555

British Library Cataloguing in Publication Data

A catalogue record for this book is available from the British Library

ISBN 978-1-4462-5892-7
ISBN 978-1-4462-5893-4 (pbk)

Contents

Foreword

During recent years there has been much public and media attention on childcare, in particular, the care and support of vulnerable children.

Foster care is an important way in which society attempts to help very vulnerable children, and key to this being a positive and productive experience for the child are the foster parents. But behind the scenes is always a supervising social worker whose role starts with the assessment of prospective foster parents through to the supervision and support of foster carers.

This new text by Helen Cosis Brown has been written to provide advice, support and guidance to all social workers working in – or aspiring to work in – this area of practice. As the author points out, this is an area that has previously received little academic reflection and, thus, this book is an important addition to the Post-Qualifying Social Work series.

On behalf of all social workers working in the fostering field I wish to sincerely thank Helen for the wisdom, insight and expertise she has shared with us in the pages within – this text really is a tremendously important contribution.

All the books in the Post-Qualifying Social Work series are written to inspire and support social work practice, with the ultimate aim of ensuring that vulnerable members of society experience the best possible social work service.

This is another such text written to inspire quality social work practice and I am sure that it will motivate you in your professional practice.

Professor Keith Brown
Director of the National Centre for Post-Qualifying Social Work, Bournemouth

About the author

Helen Cosis Brown is a Professor of Social Work in the Institute of Applied Social Research at the University of Bedfordshire. She worked as a social worker and a social work manager in inner London for ten years before moving into social work education. She has managed social work programmes at the University of Hertfordshire, South Bank University and Middlesex University. She acts as an independent foster carer reviewing officer and chairs a local authority fostering panel. Her publications have included social work with lesbians and gay men as well as fostering and adoption. Her recent publications include: Brown, HC and Cocker, C (2011) *Social Work with Lesbians and Gay Men.* London: Sage, and Brown, HC (2011) *Foster Carer Reviews: Process, Practicalities and Best Practice.* London: BAAF. She sits on a Department of Education advisory panel evaluating multidimensional treatment foster care.

Acknowledgements

My thanks to the following people whose advice and knowledge have been invaluable: Kate Alibone, Sue Anderson, Maria Boffey, Sarah Borthwick, Christine Cocker, Elaine Dibben, Phyllis Elwood, Ena Fry, Wendy Gill, Hazel Halle, Joy Howard, Maureen Ingham, Alison King, Ravi Kohli, Jacqui Lawrence, Freda Lewis, Sarah Lewis-Brooke, Meral Mehmet, Frances Nicholson, Linda Norwood, Doreen Price, Ruth Richards, Jeremy Rosenblatt, Diana Searle, Philip Sutton, Alice Twaite, Philippa Williams and Lynn Woodhouse.

I would like to acknowledge the help I have received from the following organisations: the National Society for the Prevention of Cruelty to Children's Library; the Wales, Scotland, Northern Ireland and London Fostering Network offices; and the Wales, Scotland, Northern Ireland and London BAAF offices.

I want to acknowledge, and record, the excellent social work and foster care practice I have observed, and been engaged with, through my recent involvement with the following fostering services: Greater London Fostering, the London Borough of Bromley and the London Borough of Southwark. Being involved in different capacities with these three organisations has helped me learn from others, both social workers and foster carers, and develop my practice and thinking.

Thanks also go to the panel members of the four fostering panels I have chaired since 1998, and the members of the current fostering panel I chair.

I wish to acknowledge that the British Association for Adoption and Fostering gave permission for parts of Brown, HC (2011) *Good Practice Guide to Foster Carer Reviews: Process, Practicalities and Best Practice,* London: BAAF to be reproduced in this book. Learning Matters also gave permission for parts of Brown, HC (2011) 'Foster care: learning from research and inquiries', in C Cocker and L Allain (Eds), *Advanced Social Work with Children and Families: A Post-qualifying Guide,* Exeter: Learning Matters, pp89–104 to be reproduced in this book.

Thanks also to Luke Block and Lauren Simpson from Sage/Learning Matters, and Caroline Watson from Swales & Willis, for their helpful support throughout the writing and publication process.

Lastly, I want to note the support of my family: Rebecca Swift, Aaron Brown, Casey Ryan and Veronica Lussier.

Chapter 1
Introduction

The focus of this book is social work and foster care. The book's primary, but not sole, focus is the role of the foster carer's supervising social worker (SSW). I wanted to write about the interrelationship between foster care and social work because, other than best practice guidance, the interface between the two has attracted little research, or scholarly attention. The intended readers of the book are: SSWs, foster carers, fostering service managers, students on a qualifying or post-qualifying social work degree, foster children's social workers or managers in children's social services.

Goodyer writes:

> As with other areas of social work, knowledge about fostering comes from a variety of sources: practice wisdom, individual retrospective accounts, rhetoric about what ought to happen, and also from research.

> (Goodyer, 2011, p49)

This book is a contribution to the 'knowledge' we have about social work and foster care, and falls into Goodyer's category of 'rhetoric about what ought to happen'; informed by relevant published 'knowledge', and my practice experience prior to 1989 and since 2005.

I approached writing the book from three perspectives, informed by my experience of: first, chairing fostering panels since 1998; second, chairing foster carer reviews, as an independent reviewing officer since 2005; and third as a social work academic since 1989. In writing the book I have drawn from research findings, scholarly texts, best practice guidance, and mine and others' practice experience. My theoretical orientation draws on psychodynamic understanding, systemic ideas and social learning theory to inform specific interventions.

Foster care

It is generally agreed that human beings have been 'doing' foster care, in the sense that adults have cared for other people's children, when those children have not been able to live with their birth parents, for millennia. However, the start of 'formal', paid fostering is unclear; *the origins of fostering are confused and obscured by the mists of history* (Thomas and Philpot, 2009, p15). Foster care's explicit naming, categorisation and regulation are more recent than the 'mists of history'. Smith writes:

> The foundations of foster care in the United Kingdom (UK) lie in the apprenticeships that were established by means of the Poor Law of 1536 and the practice of wet nursing that emerged during the early part of the 19th century.

> (Smith, 2011, p9)

The beginnings of the formalisation of foster care, as we would recognise it today, have been associated with the use of foster carers by: the Thomas Coram Foundling Hospital established in 1741; Reverend Armistead in Cheshire in 1853; Mrs Hannah Archer in Swindon around the same time; Dr Barnardo; and Thomas Bowman Stephenson, who was the founder of Action for Children, the then National Children's Home and Orphanage. Foster care in the late nineteenth century had become so ubiquitous that, for example, by 1891 a third of children cared for by Barnardo's were fostered (Thomas and Philpot, 2009).

Barnardo's, early on in the development of foster care, had its own equivalent to the later Government Boarding-out Regulations, to make sure that children were kept safe in foster homes. Echoes of these early regulations can be identified in the United Kingdom's (UK) 1933, 1947, 1955, 1988 and 2002, and England's 2011 and 2013 Regulations governing foster care. In each, reference was made to fostering services (or their then equivalent) being required to assess a person's 'suitability' to foster children. The need to assess 'suitability' was triggered, in part, by the 'baby farming' scandals of the nineteenth century, and the hanging of Margaret Waters in 1870 for the murder of one of the children she fostered for payment. The need to comprehensively assess prospective foster carers was re-visited by Sir Walter Monkton in his inquiry report, after the death of Dennis O'Neill, killed by his foster parents in 1945 (Home Office, 1945).

In recent research about people's motivations to foster, and barriers that prevent them fostering, concern about the stigma still associated with foster care, and a person receiving payment for caring for other people's children, was identified as a barrier for some people applying to be foster carers. Worries about being seen to profit from caring for children remains a barrier for some people applying to be foster carers (McDermid, Holmes, Kirton and Signoretta, 2012, p6). This concern can be traced back to the above events in foster care's history, which remain in our collective memories.

From a non-State controlled beginning, foster care has been transformed, in recent times, into a highly regulated activity. We currently have a mixed economy of providers of foster care including local authorities, not-for-profit and for-profit fostering services (Sellick, 2011).

Foster carers now receive regular supervision from their SSWs, to ensure that they work effectively with others responsible for the realisation of a foster child's care plan: providing a warm, facilitative, stimulating, family environment, and the enabling direct care needed to help that foster child reach their potential and be well cared for during their time in foster care. Today foster care can provide both a secure base for a child, and what I refer to as 'reparatory family care', when that is needed. Foster care, at its most basic function, is a form of 'accommodation' for children who are looked after, and at its best is an intervention in a child's life that can potentially make a significant difference for the better.

How this book is structured

The book is made up of seven substantive chapters, all of which relate to different aspects of social work and foster care. Six of the chapters have illustrative case studies which are fictitious, but informed by my practice experience since 2005.

Two points need explaining to the reader. First, I refer to foster carer in the singular, in the main, for ease of reading, but am aware that most fostering households are comprised of couples who foster. Second, like many local authorities are increasingly doing, I refer to 'child looked after', with its related acronym, CLA, thus avoiding the much criticised shortening of the term 'looked after child' to LAC; an unfortunate acronym, being so close as it is to 'lack', a word we would not want associated with children in public care.

Chapter 2 gives the reader an overview of the legal and policy landscape that foster care and social work inhabit. The rate of change regarding legislative and policy developments in this area of practice is formidable; what is covered in the chapter relates to the time of writing. It was beyond the scope of this book to cover the legislative frameworks for foster care in all four nations of the UK; this chapter only addresses that of England. However, the substance of the rest of the book is relevant to social work and foster care practice in all four UK nations.

Chapter 3 considers seven inquiries and serious case reviews (SCR) involving the deaths of, or injury to, children while in foster care. From the findings of the related reports the chapter draws together matters relating to: the regulatory framework; the assessment process; inter-professional communication; resources; and skills acquisition or application.

Chapter 4 addresses the assessment of prospective foster carers and includes discussion about: recruitment of foster carers; types of foster care; assessment in general; assessment of foster carers in particular; what the Standards, Guidance and Regulations say; what needs to be considered in all foster carer assessments; tools for undertaking assessments; assessing sameness and difference; recruiting and assessing particular groups of foster carers; ethnicity, nationality and religion; and the assessment of lesbian and gay prospective foster carers.

Chapter 5 discusses the supervision and support of foster carers. Here the role of the SSW is explicitly examined. What the Standards, Guidance and Regulations say; the SSW/foster carer supervisory relationship; supervision; support and development; child-focused reparatory care; placement planning; team around the child; contact; foster children moving on; managing allegations; valuing and developing a child's heritage/positive sense of self; and permanence are all considered.

Chapter 6 examines what we know about the support and development of foster carers and the SSW role. The following are explored: the Skills to Foster preparation training programme; personal development plans (PDP); the Training Support and Development Standards (TSDS); what the research tells us about the effectiveness of training for foster carers; Fostering Changes; Multidimensional Treatment Foster Care (MTFC)/Keeping Foster Parents Trained and Supported, KEEP; and foster carer support groups.

Chapter 7 argues for the need for fostering services to place particular emphasis on foster carer reviews, as a mechanism through which each individual foster carer's practice can be developed and foster care enhanced more generally. This chapter covers: what the Standards, Guidance and Regulations say; the review administrative process; the SSW's report; facilitating contributors' input into foster carer reviews; and the review meeting.

Chapter 8 looks at fostering panels, and specifically: the related regulatory framework; foster carers, SSWs and reviewing officers attending fostering panels; approvals; matching; and reviews.

The main message that I hope to convey in this book is that foster care can make a beneficial difference to children's lives, and that the role of the SSW is fundamental to making this happen.

Chapter 2

The legal and policy framework for foster care

CHAPTER OBJECTIVES

By the end of this chapter, readers should:

- be familiar with and understand the legal and policy framework for social work and foster care in England;
- be able to consider how the legal and policy framework for foster care can be utilised by you, as a social worker, to enhance the quality of foster carers' and foster children's lives.

Introduction

I start this chapter with a pertinent quote from a young person who was interviewed as part of the Care Inquiry (2013), reminding us that a legal framework, which is fit for purpose, alone does not necessarily guarantee good outcomes for foster children:

> I think what's important is for the Government to stop making new laws and work instead with what we have already and try and develop it for the better. What's important is for them to try and find ways of catering for all of us as individuals so that we grow up and become successful young people who were in care, not young people who are not successful because they were in care.
>
> (Care Inquiry, 2013, p24)

A similar message was conveyed to the UK Government some 68 years before by Sir Walter Monkton, the author of the Dennis O'Neill Inquiry (Home Office, 1945), when he suggested that further regulatory change was not what was needed to safeguard foster children. He believed that the then 1933 Boarding-out Regulations (Home Office, 1933) were still fit for purpose and that, rather than instigating change, *their requirement should be treated as a minimum, not a barely attainable maximum* (Home Office, 1945, p18).

However, relentless changes in the last 60 years to legal regulation and social services' organisational structures, relating to social work with children and families, are, in part, testament to the words of neither Sir Monkton nor the young person giving evidence to the Care Inquiry being heeded. The legislative frameworks for children looked after by the State, and foster care, have been in a regular state of flux since 1945. The seeming belief that changing the detail of the law, and the structure of organisations, will improve children's life chances, rather than addressing why such changes have not, in the last 68 years, in the main led to radically improved outcomes for children for whom the State acts as the corporate parent, has been a hallmark of children and families social policy in the UK. However, an interruption to this pattern more recently, in the field of child protection, was the Government-commissioned report (Munro, 2011), which tried to address some of the more complex matters relating to social work with children and families, about social work practice itself, among other matters.

Laws, regulations, guidance and standards provide a framework for what must be, as well as what can be done. However, as noted above, legal regulation cannot by itself safeguard foster children's interests. As Brammer writes:

> *Policies, legislation, structures and procedures are, of course, of immense importance, but they serve only as a means of securing better life opportunities for each young person. It is the robust and consistent implementation of these policies and procedures which keeps children and young people safe.*

> (Brammer, 2010, p166)

In other words, it is the quality of the implementation of law, regulations, guidance and standards that makes a difference to young people and children who are fostered.

Following the Conservative and Liberal Democrat Coalition Government coming to power in May 2010, the new Government continued the work started by the previous Labour Government, regarding improving the quality of the lives of children looked after, and foster care. The outputs of this work were the current Standards, Guidance and Regulations governing foster care which came into force in 2011, replacing those that had been in place since 2002. However, no sooner than the 2011 Standards, Guidance and Regulations for foster care were in place, and before it was possible to see if they made a difference to the quality of foster carers' and foster children's lives, the Government embarked on an 'improving foster care agenda' (Department of Education, 2012a; Harber and Oakley, 2012). This new agenda was, in part, in recognition that the State still had a long way to go before foster children as a group, rather than individual foster children, who often do extremely well, could be said to be thriving. Harber and Oakley remind us that foster care is still not realising the positive potential of many children, and argue that reform of foster care is still needed to enable foster children to thrive:

> *They are not being lifted to achieve everything that we should hope that they do. Evidence of these poor outcomes is easy to find:*
>
> - *Around half of children in care have been diagnosed with a mental disorder;*
> - *Educational outcomes are appalling, with only around a third of children in care achieving the expected Key Stage 2 level in English and Maths (compared to 74 per cent in the general population of children);*

- *Twice as many 19 year olds who were previously in the care system are now not in education, employment or training (33 per cent) than for the general 19-year-old population (16 per cent); and over the longer-term, over a quarter of all adults serving custodial sentences previously spent time in care and almost half of all under 21 year olds in contact with the criminal justice system have spent time in care.*

It is a tragedy that the 48,530 children currently in foster care in England are at risk of poor outcomes and life chances.

(Harber and Oakley, 2012, p8)

At the time of writing some aspects of the Government's 'improving foster care' initiative had come to fruition, but others, such as guidance on long-term foster care and commissioning of foster care placements, were still being developed. 'Fostering for adoption', a development introduced in the Children and Families Bill 2013, is already having an impact on, and implications for, fostering services (Department of Education, 2013a; Simmonds, 2013).

There are a number of texts that cover law relevant to social work, children looked after and foster care (Brammer, 2010; Davis, 2010; Laird, 2010; Lawson, 2011a; Brayne and Carr, 2013). There are also a number of best practice guides that include the legal and policy framework for specific areas of foster care. These include: fostering panels (Borthwick and Lord, 2011); foster carer reviews (Brown, 2011); parent and child fostering (Adams and Dibben, 2011) and fostering for adoption (Simmonds, 2013). Specific areas of the legal and policy framework for foster care will be re-visited in more detail throughout the book where relevant.

Lawson lists the legislation and guidance relevant to foster care in England (Lawson, 2011a, pp9–11) and reminds us that *the regulations, statutory guidance and NMS are not just relevant to staff of fostering services: it is essential that everyone who works with children and young people in foster care is aware of what they say* (2011a, p9). Knowledge of the law can enable social workers to facilitate good quality foster care, and inform them about how to use the law as leverage, to ensure foster carers, foster children and their families receive the services, safeguards and quality of support to which they are entitled by law.

In the UK, legislation about the welfare of children and young people focuses on the best interests of children. This is stated in primary legislation in England, Wales, Scotland and Northern Ireland. The Children (Northern Ireland) Order 1995, the Children Act (Scotland) 1995, the Children Act 1989 and the Children Act 2004 all state that children's welfare has to be the paramount consideration. This also has to be the case for foster care. The welfare of a specific foster child, or a hypothetical foster child that might be placed with a foster carer in the future, has to be the paramount consideration for social workers.

This chapter covers

- The legal and policy framework in which social work and foster care take place. It sets out the current legal and policy landscapes for foster care. This legal landscape is an ever-changing terrain and the chapter reflects it as it was at the time of writing. The foster care Standards, Regulations and Guidance are briefly introduced, as well as other relevant secondary legislation.

- The specific detail of each document is not covered, but rather the chapter signposts the reader to documents with which they should be familiar, if they are social workers working with foster carers or foster children.

- The chapter starts by considering the UKNSFC (UK Joint Working Party on Foster Care, 1999a) and the related Code of Practice on the recruitment, assessment, approval, training, management and support of foster carers (UK Joint Working Party on Foster Care, 1999b). Both these documents apply to the UK as a whole, but are not legally binding. However, although now dated, they still offer direction regarding best practice in foster care.

The UK National Standards for foster care, and the Code of Practice

These two publications apply to all four UK nations (UK Joint Working Party on Foster Care, 1999a; UK Joint Working Party on Foster Care, 1999b). They were the first attempt, in the UK, to create a Code of Practice and National Standards for foster care. Mehmet, writing about the UK National Standards and Code of Practice, wrote:

> *These two documents set out to establish what was to be expected from everyone involved in foster care, the fostering teams, children's social workers and carers. The work of the Joint Working Party on Foster Care which produced these documents opened the way for Standards in foster care to be recognised across the United Kingdom.*

> (Mehmet, 2005, p3)

The English, Scottish and Welsh Governments subsequently published their own national standards for foster care (Department of Education, 2011a; The Scottish Executive, 2005; Welsh Assembly Government, 2003). Wales, Scotland and Northern Ireland have all developed their own Code of Practice (Wales Code of Practice Working Group, 1999; The Scottish Executive and the Fostering Network, 2004; Department of Health and Social Service, 1999). Although the UKNSFC and Code of Practice were not legally binding, they did in effect establish best practice guidance in foster care. They remain helpful detailed documents about foster care and social work practice and are worth practitioners' and social work students' attention.

Policy, Standards, Regulation and Guidance relating to foster care in general

The documents below are introduced to the reader in a, hopefully, logical order, but not necessarily chronologically. I start with the White Paper, Care Matters, as this set the tone for the foster care reform agenda that followed. I then move on to the Standards, Regulation and Guidance because these, taken together, are the bedrock of the legal framework for foster care.

Care Matters: Time for Change

The White Paper Care Matters, published by the Department for Education and Skills in 2007, sought to improve the lots of, and futures for, children in public care. Central to this agenda was improving the quality and stability of foster care and the status of foster carers. *Foster carers are central to many children and young people's experience of care. It is essential that we value and support them and ensure that they are properly equipped with the necessary range of skills* (Department for Education and Skills, 2007, pp8–9). One initiative related to this was the Children's Workforce Development Council's (CWDC) creation in 2007 of the Training, Support and Development Standards for Foster Care (TSDS). When the Conservative/Liberal Democrat Coalition Government came to power in 2010, and subsequently the CWDC was abolished, the TSDS were, as a result, adopted by the Department of Education, and Guidance was re-issued in 2012 by the Department of Education.

The Fostering Services: National Minimum Standards

The Department of Education published the Fostering Services: National Minimum Standards (NMS) in 2011 under Section 23 of the Care Standards Act 2000. The NMS set out the expectations for the standards that must be met by fostering services (Department of Education, 2011a; Dunster, 2011; Lawson, 2011a). There are 31 Standards, which include child-focused Standards (Standards 1–12), as well as Standards for the fostering service (Standards 13–31). The Standards for the fostering service include some subjects covered in the following chapters of this book including: recruiting and assessing foster carers (Standard 13); fostering panels (Standard 14); learning and development of foster carers (Standard 20); supervision and support of foster carers (Standard 21); handling allegations (Standard 22); and placements plans and their review (Standard 31).

Fostering Services (England) Regulations

These Regulations were published by the Department of Education in 2011 (Department of Education, 2011b; Dunster, 2011; Lawson, 2011a). They set out the regulatory framework for foster care in England and, pertinent to social work and foster care, cover: the assessment and approval of foster carers; foster carer reviews; termination of foster carers' approval; and fostering panels. The Independent Review Mechanism's (IRM) relationship to foster carers' approval, review, the fostering panel and the fostering service is also noted. These Regulations, as they related to assessment and approval of foster carers, were amended in 2013 by the Department of Education (Department of Education, 2013b).

Assessment and approval of foster carers: Amendments to the Children Act 1989 Guidance and Regulations

The Amendments (Department of Education, 2013b) set out the new two-stage process for the assessment of prospective foster carers, which is elaborated upon in Chapter 4 of this book, as well as a number of miscellaneous matters including: the sharing of information for the purposes of foster carer or adopter assessments; the IRM; the usual fostering limit; reviews and terminations of approval of foster carers; and the role of the Agency Decision Maker (ADM).

The Children Act 1989 Guidance and Regulations Volume 4: Fostering Services

The Children Act 1989 Guidance and Regulations Volume 4 (HM Government, 2011), taken with the NMS (Department of Education, 2011a) and the Fostering Service (England) Regulations (Department of Education, 2011b), form the regulatory framework for fostering services in England (Dunster, 2011; Lawson, 2011a). Volume 4 provides the detail of what is expected of good quality foster care. Sections of this volume will be revisited in forthcoming chapters in this book, for example, what is meant by 'delegated authority', and what this means for social work with foster carers (HM Government, 2011, p15).

The Children Act 1989 Guidance and Regulations Volume 2: Care Planning, Placement and Case Review 2010

HM Government's Guidance and Regulations Volume 2 were published by the Department for Children, Schools and Families in 2010. They were part of the implementation of the Care Matters White Paper, and the Children and Young Persons Act 2008. Volume 2 provides Guidance and Regulations regarding care planning, case review and the placement of children who are looked after. In the assessment of prospective foster carers and their subsequent reviews, the careful evaluation of what they can be expected to, as well as want to, have as their terms of approval is noted in Volume 2 as follows:

> *Foster carer assessments are designed to identify the ages, number or needs of the children to whom the foster carer is most likely to offer the best care. Research evidence consistently shows that placements outside the terms of approval are significantly more likely to result in placement breakdown, often if there is a foster child already in the household. Where the responsible authority wishes to amend the terms of approval to enable the child to remain with the*

carer, careful consideration must be made by the fostering panel to ensure that the carer has the capacity to meet the child's needs in the context of the needs of other children in the household.

(HM Government, 2010, p57)

A social worker's assessment of a foster carer's capacity to care for particular categories of children at the approval stage, and re-assessment of the appropriateness of a foster carer's terms of approval, as time goes on, is particularly important. This re-assessment is part of the foster carer review process and should be carefully considered at each review (Brown, 2011).

Importantly, the Guidance and Regulations Volume 2 sets out what is expected of children's social workers in respect of placement planning. This was further strengthened through the 2013 amendments (Department of Education, 2013c).

Delegation of Authority: Amendments to the Children Act 1989 Guidance and Regulations Volume 2: Care Planning, Placement and Case Review

The amendments (Department of Education, 2013c) helpfully firm up the expectations placed on local authorities and fostering services in respect of the delegation of authority from those with parental responsibility to the foster carer, to enable foster children to live as ordinary lives as possible. The amendments note that delegated authority should be clarified in the placement plan for each foster child.

Regulation and guidance relating to specific areas of foster care

The following Regulations and Guidance relate to particular types or aspects of foster care, as well as requirements placed on local authorities to sustain enough foster carer placements for children needing foster care, and lastly training and development requirements for foster carers.

The Care Planning, Placement and Case Review and Fostering Services (England) (Miscellaneous Amendments) Regulations

These Regulations were published by the Department of Education in 2013, and cover the temporary approval of prospective adopters as foster carers (Department of Education, 2013a). The Coram Centre for Early Permanence and the British Association for Adoption and Fostering (BAAF) have since published helpful guidance for social workers and local authorities about fostering for adoption (Simmonds, 2013).

Family and friends care: statutory guidance for local authorities

The Department of Education published this Guidance in 2010 (Department of Education, 2010a). The Guidance sets out what is expected of local authorities regarding the temporary approval of a 'connected person' to care for a child looked after. It also covers the requirements of the full assessment of a family and friends foster carer (connected person), which should be completed within sixteen weeks, and in exceptional cases a further eight weeks can be allowed once the local authority's 'nominated officer' has consulted the fostering panel and the independent reviewing officer for the child.

The Guidance has a more generally useful Annex A, setting out the legal framework for: private fostering; family care (informal); family and friends foster care; unrelated foster care; residence orders; special guardianship orders and adoption. For each of these the following are considered: route into the caring arrangement; parental responsibility; approval basis; duration; placement supervision; review of placement; support services; financial support – entitlement; and financial support – discretionary (Department of Education, 2010a, pp41–3).

Private fostering

This book does not look specifically at private fostering, but for the benefit of the reader I have included here references regarding private fostering Regulations (Department for Education and Skills, 2005a), Guidance on private fostering (Department for Education and Skills, 2005b) and the National Minimum Standards for private fostering (Department for Education and Skills, 2005c), for information.

The Children Act 1989 Guidance and Regulations Volume 3: Planning Transition to Adulthood for Care Leavers Including the Care Leavers (England) Regulations 2010

The Guidance and Regulations were published by the Department of Education in 2010 (Department of Education, 2010b), the Government's intention being to:

Ensure care leavers are given the same level of care and support that their peers would expect from a reasonable parent and that they are provided with the opportunities and chances needed to help them move successfully to adulthood. Research and practice show that those leaving care supported according to the following principles have the best chance of successful transition to adulthood: quality; giving chances where needed; tailoring to individuals' needs. The Guidance seeks to have these principles at the centre of decision making for care leavers.

(Department of Education, 2010b, p1)

The Government's objectives regarding care leavers were further enhanced by the 'Staying Put' initiative, enabling fostered young people to remain with their foster carers after their 18th birthday, until such time that they are ready to live independently.

'STAYING PUT': Arrangements for care leavers aged 18 and above to stay on with their former foster carers, Department of Education, DWP and HMRC Guidance

The above Guidance was published by the Department of Education in 2013 (HM Government, 2013a). The Guidance states that the intention of 'Staying Put' is:

To ensure young people can remain with their former foster carers until they are prepared for adulthood, can experience a transition akin to their peers, avoid social exclusion and be more likely to avert a subsequent housing and tenancy breakdown.

(HM Government, 2013a, p4)

This Guidance sets out the necessary mechanisms required to enable this staged transition to happen for young people after the age of 18 years who have been foster children.

Short breaks: statutory guidance on how to safeguard and promote the welfare of disabled children using short breaks

This Guidance was published by the Department for Children, Schools and Families in 2010 (Department for Children, Schools and Families, 2010a), and sought to make sure that disabled children were offered good quality short breaks away from their families, to enable those families to have a break, and for that break to be experienced by a child as a positive time spent with another family with whom they become familiar. The Guidance looks at the use of foster carers for such breaks, alongside other provisions such as residential care.

The document brings together into one volume all the existing and new statutory Guidance relevant to the provision of short breaks for disabled children and their families. The main elements are:

- *short breaks and the provision of accommodation;*

- *assessment, planning, implementation and review cycle for children using short breaks; and*

- *the different settings in which short breaks may take place.*

(Department for Children, Schools and Families, 2010a, p3)

'Separated children', unaccompanied migrant children and young people

Unlike Wales (All Wales Child Protection Procedures Review Group, 2011), England does not currently have Department of Education Guidance on working with separated children. However, we do have the House of Lords, House of Commons Joint Committee on Human Rights' first report of the 2013–2014 session (2013). This report addresses the human rights of unaccompanied migrant children and young people in the UK, and is therefore pertinent for foster carers and social workers working with separated children.

Sufficiency statutory guidance on securing sufficient accommodation for looked after children

The Department for Children, Schools and Families published this Guidance in 2010 (Department for Children Schools and Families, 2010b) with the intention of making sure that local authorities had enough placements in their locality to meet the needs of children they looked after. This has remained an area of difficulty, hence the Department of Education returning to the thorny issue of commissioning foster placements in their improving foster care agenda in 2013.

Training, Support and Development Standards for foster care

The Department of Education published Guidance in 2012 about the TSDS for 'general' foster carers (Department of Education, 2012b), family and friends foster carers (Department of Education, 2012c), short breaks foster carers (Department of Education, 2012d) and support foster carers (Department of Education, 2012e). These Standards complement the NMS (Department of Education, 2011a) but are specific to training, support and development of foster carers. There are seven Standards that foster carers have to meet within the first year of their approval.

Additional relevant guidance

All Guidance associated with children who are looked after will also be relevant to foster carers and their SSWs. Such Guidance includes: Promoting the Educational Achievement of Looked After Children (Department for Children, Schools and Families, 2010c); Promoting the Health and Well-Being of Looked After Children (Department for Children, Schools and Families, 2009); Guidance for Independent Reviewing Officers and Local Authorities on Their Functions in Relation to Case Management and Review (Department for Children, Schools and Families, 2010d) and Working Together to Safeguard Children: A Guide to Inter-agency Working to Safeguard and Promote the Welfare of Children (HM Government, 2013b).

The Foster Carers' Charter

I end this chapter with the Foster Carers' Charter (Department of Education, 2011c), which is neither Guidance nor Regulation, but is included here as an important document devised by a number of organisations, and published by the Department of Education to signal the Government's goal to raise the status of foster carers, and foster care, and thus the life chances of fostered children. Tim Loughton, the Children's Minister at the time of the Charter's publication, in the Charter's foreword notes the interrelatedness of the role of foster carers and the outcomes for foster children when he writes:

> It is essential therefore that foster carers are at the heart of arrangements for looked after children and must be fully engaged, supported and consulted at every stage. Without understanding how important the role of a foster carer is and what they can expect from others, it is so much harder to do the best for these children and young people. At the same time everyone needs to be focused on what is best for the most important people of all – the children in their care.

(Department of Education, 2011c, foreword)

Fostering services, responsible for the supervision and support of foster carers, have a key role in helping foster carers be equipped to care for foster children in such a way that helps contribute to them having happy enough childhoods and potentially fulfilled lives.

Chapter summary

- England's legal framework for foster care establishes the minimum requirements below which social work and foster care practice cannot fall. The UKNSFC (UK Joint Working Party on Foster Care, 1999a) still offers a best practice framework which, although dated and not legally binding, complements the existing policy, Standards, Regulations and Guidance.

- Legal frameworks have to be understood and adhered to, but should be treated as the bare minimum, not the inspirational goal of practice. Best practice involves abiding by the letter of the law, but also developing practice that more than meets the basic legal requirements.

- As well as abiding by primary and secondary legislation and policy directives we need to learn from the relevant findings of childcare inquiries, involving foster carers, to make sure we take note of their findings and recommendations to improve social work and foster care practice (Chapter 3).

FURTHER READING

Lawson, D (2011a) *Fostering Regulations, Guidance and NMS 2011 (England)*. London: The Fostering Network.

Lawson, D (2011b) *A Foster Care Handbook for Supervising Social Workers (England)*. London: The Fostering Network.

Lawson, D (2011c) *Family and Friends Foster Care: Information for Foster Carers (England)*. London: The Fostering Network.

Together these three publications provide a comprehensive basis for understanding the legal framework for foster care up to 2011, and the role of the SSW.

Chapter 3

Recommendations arising from inquiry reports and serious case reviews (SCRs)

CHAPTER OBJECTIVES

By the end of this chapter, readers should:

- be familiar with seven inquiry and SCR reports related to foster care, written between 1945 and 2010;
- understand what the key findings were from each case;
- have an appreciation of how the learning from these cases can be utilised in social work and foster care practice today.

Introduction

Potentially, foster care offers children reparatory family life, and can make a difference to children's physical, emotional and educational development and ultimately their life chances. Chapter 2 examined England's legal, policy and regulatory framework for foster care, which aims to make sure that foster care offers children a good experience, and at worst one that is good enough. Social work and foster care practice has to conform to regulatory governance frameworks to ensure that a foster child's needs are met, their potential is realised and each child is kept safe. At the most minimal level the statutory foster care governance framework is there to safeguard foster children, as well as making sure the standards of foster care are such that they sustain safe, nurturing, stimulating family life for children.

In addition to the legislative framework governing foster care, it is important for social workers to be familiar with findings and recommendations arising from inquiry and SCR reports, when they have something to say about foster care. Individuals and society as a whole have difficulty taking on board the fact that some foster carers not only do not meet the needs of children in their care but also, in rare cases, actively harm children entrusted to them. The Department of Health, analysing child abuse inquiries of the

1980s, commented that: *The single lesson to be learned, is that child abuse takes place in foster homes, and this knowledge should affect the manner of selection, the speed of placement, and the social work contact in placement* (Department of Health, 1991, p97).

Utting addressed the complexity of this area of social work practice when he wrote:

> *Investigations into allegations of abuse in foster care or residential settings dif-fer significantly from investigations into allegations against parents or others in the child's own home. Social workers find themselves examining the actions of people regarded as co-workers or professional colleagues.*

> (Utting, 1997, p182)

Deaths and serious abuse of children in foster homes is not the norm, indeed it is rare. However, some inquiry reports and SCRs are testament to the fact that sometimes things do go seriously wrong in foster care. Most importantly these reports remind practition-ers and fostering services of the need to be rigorous in the assessment, supervision and review of foster carers.

Reder and Duncan, writing about inquiry reports relating to child deaths, not just those related to foster care, wrote: *The consistency between the findings is striking, with particular clusters around: deficiencies in the assessment process; problems with inter-professional communication; inadequate resources; and poor skills acquisition or application* (Reder and Duncan, 2004, p96). These 'clusters' are similarly borne out in the inquiry reports and SCRs involving foster carers identified in this chapter. When identify-ing themes arising from the seven inquiries and SCRs utilised here, I have adapted Reder and Duncan's 'cluster' headings as follows: *the assessment process; inter-professional communication; resources; and skills acquisition or application*, and added the regulatory framework.

There have been a number of inquiry reports and SCRs since 1945 either where a child has died while in foster care, or where they were seriously abused. The reports examined what went wrong in each of these cases, as well as making recommendations for the future, in the hope of lessening the likelihood of similar circumstances arising again. If we are to develop best practice in social work and foster care it is important that we are aware of these findings and recommendations, and our practice adapts accordingly.

Brandon, Bailey and Belderson's analysis of SCRs from 2007 to 2009 of children killed or harmed through actual or probable abuse or neglect, identified:

> *five cases involving younger children who died or were harmed while in foster and respite care. These SCRs concerned the neglect or inadequate care of chil-dren with a disability and/or complex health needs, and alleged physical assault or sexual abuse from carers.*

> (Brandon et al., 2010, p36)

Two years later Brandon, Sidebotham, Bailey, Belderson, Hawley, Ellis and Megson's anal-ysis of SCRs, for the period 2009–2011, noted the number of reviews where the death of, or serious injury to, a child occurred while the child was placed with foster carers. In these cases, because of the nature of the documents being analysed, it was not discernible whether or not the foster carer was the perpetrator in each case. What is interesting is the relatively 'small numbers' of foster children involved, compared to children living at home. Most importantly the percentage of such cases declined from 2005, as can be seen in the table below.

Table 3.1

Where living at time of incident	Frequency 2005–07 (n = 187)	Frequency 2007–09 (n = 278)	Frequency 2009–11 (n = 177)
At home	148 (79%)	229 (82%)	145 (82%)
With relatives	10 (5%)	11 (4%)	8 (5%)
With foster carers (short term, long term or short break)	7 (4%)	8 (3%)	4 (2%)
Hospital, mother and baby unit and residential children's home	7 (4%)	15 (5%)	8 (5%)
Semi-independence unit	5 (3%)	3 (1%)	1 (1%)
Other, including young offender institutions	10 (5%)	12 (4%)	11 (6%)

(Brandon *et al.*, 2012, p36)

Biehal and Parry, in their review of the evidence about the prevalence and nature of allegations of maltreatment against foster carers, conclude that *it remains unclear how many carers experience allegations of abuse and what proportion of these allegations are subsequently substantiated* (Biehal and Parry, 2010, p42).

Talking of 'small numbers', as I did above, when discussing the deaths of, or serious injury to, children while placed in foster care seems shockingly dismissive. Any avoidable death of a child in public care is utterly deplorable. At the very least, we expect children in public care to be kept alive, and free from serious injury or harm. However, quite separate from abuse perpetrated by adults, the reality of family life is that it is full of ordinary risk, and sometimes things do go very wrong in ways that might be difficult to avoid. For example, car accidents, where the fault was not that of the foster carer, happen, as was the case in 2012 when a foster carer lost her husband, mother and two foster children in a tragic car accident in Mid Wales (Crump, 2012). Also, in the home, accidents happen in non-fostering families and fostering families alike. Because of this, responsible authorities understandably spend considerable time making sure that foster homes are physically safe, and that foster children are properly supervised, to lessen the likelihood of serious accidents occurring. This diligent monitoring and inspection has to be balanced against a foster child's need/right to live as ordinary a family life as is possible, including the opportunity to take considered, calculated risks.

When children do die in foster homes, through accidents, some quarters of the press use such tragedies as an opportunity to lambast the entire care system, as was the case with the death of Anna Hider in 2007. She was 17 months old and in care to Portsmouth County Council when she drowned in her foster carers' swimming pool (Glendinning, 2007). The Daily Mail used Anna Hider's death to further their then campaign against children being removed from their parents. At the time two journalists wrote:

> *The case again throws the spotlight onto the care system and the apparent ease with which children can be taken from their birth parents.*
>
> *It is less than a week since a Daily Mail special report outlined how dozens of children are allegedly being taken from their parents to be placed for adoption, often on the back of the flimsiest of allegations and, at times, mere hearsay.*

(Fernandez and Dolan, 2007)

The point the *Daily Mail* and Anna Hider's birth parents were able to exploit was that if Portsmouth County Council had not removed Anna from her mother, the chances were that she would have remained alive.

Such accidents, whether they are car crashes, drowning or death or injury by other means, are risks that beset all families, fostering families included. Some risks associated with family life can be minimised by proportionate and reasonable care being exercised by the foster carer, the SSW and the fostering service, without preventing children enjoying the full range of activities that we want them to experience in a family placement.

This chapter, rather than addressing 'accidents', considers seven cases where harm was deliberately perpetrated by those adults to whom local authorities had entrusted foster children. I have selected the following to consider: the Dennis O'Neill Inquiry (Home Office, 1945); the Shirley Woodcock Inquiry (Hammersmith and Fulham, 1984); the Derbyshire and Nottinghamshire Inquiry (Derbyshire and Nottinghamshire, 1990); the Wakefield Inquiry (Parrott, MacIver and Thoburn, 2007); the Serious Case Review of Mrs Spry (Gloucestershire Safeguarding Children Board, 2008); the Serious Case Review of child V and Mr and Mrs A (Rotherham Safeguarding Children Board, 2009); and the overview report on Mr and Mrs B (Rotherham Safeguarding Children Board, 2010). This is by no means an exhaustive list. These seven reports cover a 65-year span, which means that the social, social care and social work contexts differ between them; for example, the Dennis O'Neill Inquiry report of 1945 and the overview report on Mr and Mrs B of 2010 were written within their own social and historical contexts. I have covered such a broad time span because some of the messages have remained consistent, and we therefore still need to heed the reports' findings and recommendations. The inquiry report looking at all aspects of foster care in most depth is the Wakefield Inquiry (Parrott *et al.*, 2007). I have not covered reports that considered the deaths of children placed with prospective adopters, as this book's focus is on social work and foster care.

This chapter covers

- Inquiry reports and SCRs 1945–2010
    - o The Dennis O'Neill Inquiry
    - o The Shirley Woodcock Inquiry

- o The Derbyshire and Nottinghamshire Inquiry
- o The Wakefield Inquiry
- o The Serious Case Review of Mrs Spry
- o The Serious Case Review of child V and Mr and Mrs A
- o The overview report on Mr and Mrs B.

- Learning from inquiry and SCR reports
  - o The regulatory framework
  - o The assessment process
  - o Inter-professional communication
  - o Resources
  - o Skills acquisition or application.

Inquiry reports and SCRs 1945–2010

It is beyond the remit of this book to go into the full detail of the circumstances and recommendations of each case. Rather I have selected areas that are relevant to the role of the social worker. I look at each report in date order and then draw together from all seven reports' findings relevant to social work and foster care.

Dennis O'Neill

Dennis (12) and his brothers Terrance (9) and Fredrick (7) were in the care of Monmouth County Council. Dennis and Terrance were placed with Mr and Mrs Gough at Bank Farm, Minsterley in Shropshire; this was their third foster care placement since being taken into care in 1940. Dennis was placed with the Goughs on 28 June 1944, and Terrance joined him on 5 July 1944. Dennis died on 9 January 1945. Reginald Gough was subsequently found guilty of manslaughter, and received a six-year prison sentence, and Esther Gough was found guilty of neglect and received a six-month prison sentence. The inquiry report recounted the serious injuries found on Dennis, and the degree of neglect and undernourishment he had experienced (Home Office, 1945). Dennis was placed with the Goughs for just over six months.

The inquiry report commented on the acute shortage of foster carers and county council staff to undertake the supervision of placements at the time Dennis and Terrance were placed at Bank Farm. It noted that the Goughs had not been thoroughly assessed or references properly sought, and that not all the rooms of the house had been considered as to their suitability for fostering. Sir Monkton, the report's author, commented upon the problematic nature of relying solely on one person's assessment regarding a person's suitability to be a foster carer. He wrote that the assessor's *opinion ought to have been supplemented by inquiries from other sources* (Home Office, 1945, p10). He also noted that checks were not carried out that might have alerted the authorities to Mrs Gough having, in 1942, applied to the Wem Justices for a Separation Order, because she had experienced *persistent cruelty* at the hands of Mr Gough and that he had been previously convicted of assault.

The report identified inadequate communication between the two councils involved regarding who was responsible for the supervision of the foster home and the children. There was wrangling over levels of remuneration for the foster carers, Monmouth paying a higher rate, and Shropshire fearing that other Shropshire foster carers would become disgruntled if they became aware that the Goughs were on a higher rate of payment. The then Boarding-out Regulations requirements, related to the 1933 Children and Young Persons Act, for visits to children boarded out with foster carers were not met, indeed no visits took place between 28 June and 10 December 1944. At one point both councils had children placed with the Goughs, but neither was aware that that was the case. When they did eventually realise, the Shropshire children (the Mullinders) were moved to other foster carers in October 1944. The two Shropshire Council staff who originally placed the Mullinder siblings with the Goughs on 12 July 1944 reported that they thought the Goughs' farm house was *very bare, comfortless and isolated* (Home Office, 1945, p11). However, the Shropshire Council member of staff who had undertaken the assessment of the Goughs was of a different view, and declared herself to be *definitely satisfied with the house* (Home Office, 1945, p11).

Dennis and Terrance went to a school in Hope, where their attendance tailed off in November and December 1944. Neither child was seen by a doctor during their placement. When eventually a Newport Council officer (Mrs Edwards) visited the children on 20 December 1944 she realised that the placement was not satisfactory and described Dennis as looking *ill and frightened* (Home Office, 1945, p14). She *saw little affection on the part of the Goughs for the children* (Home Office, 1945, p14). She asked Mrs Gough to take Dennis to a doctor that day. She did not interview the children separately from the Goughs, neither did she ask to look around the house or see the children's bedroom. The same day she recommended that the children should be immediately removed. However, for a number of reasons, including serious flaws in communication between and within the two councils, the children were not removed and Dennis died on 9 January 1945, having not seen a doctor after Mrs Edwards' visit of 20 December 1944.

Similar to many subsequent inquiry reports and SCRs, a feature of this case was the shortage of staff to adequately cover the duties assigned to them. However, Sir Monkton did not find that resource constraints explained the failings of the local authority with responsibility for the children, and he wrote: *When all allowance is made for over-work and under-staffing and illness and accident, the plain fact remains that they failed in selection and supervision of the foster home* (Home Office, 1945, p16).

Sir Monkton concluded the 1933 Children and Young Persons Act and the 1933 Rules for Boarding-out Poor Law Children were adequate but the practice and administration in the case were not. He wrote:

> *What is required is rather that the administrative machinery should be improved and informed by a more anxious and responsible spirit . . . The boarding-out rules ought plainly to be obeyed in the letter and the spirit. Their requirement should be treated as a minimum, not a barely attainable maximum.*

> (Home Office, 1945, p18)

Despite Sir Monkton's conclusion that the legislation and regulations did not, in his view, contribute to Dennis O'Neill's death, his report was one of the contributory factors leading to the setting up of the Curtis Committee (Curtis, 1946), which laid the ground for the Children Act 1948 and the 1947 Home Office and Ministry of Health Regulations on the boarding-out of children (Corby, Doig and Roberts, 2001). Indeed rather than noting Monkton's counsel that increasing bureaucracy and regulation would not necessarily improve the protection of children, since then the reverse has in fact been the case as noted by Parton:

> *What becomes evident, however, is that at each stage of revision the Guidance has become longer, more detailed and more complex; including the revision following Lord Laming's Inquiry Report into the death of Victoria Climbié (HM Government, 2006). This is, therefore, a particular challenge for anyone wishing to reform the child protection system in England in order to free it 'from unnecessary bureaucracy and regulation'.*

> (Parton, 2011, p4)

The Dennis O'Neill Inquiry marked the start of a pattern of anxious tinkering with the legislative and procedural frameworks and organisational structures in response to child deaths.

Shirley Woodcock

Shirley died on 4 April 1982 aged 3 years and 3 months, while placed with foster carers. This placement was her third since she went into care. Shirley and her brother (4) were placed with their foster carers on 10 December 1981. Both children had considerable emotional needs, which, the inquiry report concluded, were more than their foster mother could manage. At the time that Shirley and her brother were placed with the foster carers, there was a shortage of foster carers in the borough and the inquiry team questioned the probity of matching these children, whose needs were extensive, with these particular foster carers. The foster carers themselves, by November 1981, asked for the children to be removed *saying that they were a bit too much for them* (Hammersmith and Fulham, 1984, p60). The report identified areas pertinent to this book as follows: the Boarding-Out of Children Regulations 1955 were not adhered to; inadequate supervision of the assessor during the assessment of the foster carers; some of the social workers' visits to the family were not recorded; there was fundamental disagreement between the fostering team and the team responsible for the child, the former thinking that Shirley and her brother should be moved from the placement, and the latter that a further move would be too disruptive for them; the foster mother described Shirley as being a 'faddy eater' whereas the same child had recently been described as having a good appetite; marks and scratches were noticed on Shirley by a fostering officer on 28 January 1982 on a home visit and at that time Shirley was wetting herself, soiling and had sleep problems; on 16 March a child-minding visitor noticed a row of bruises around Shirley's neck which the foster mother explained as being self-inflicted; a health visitor who saw Shirley on 19 March 1982 noted that there were problems in the placement. Around this time Shirley's nursery also reported bruising. None of these factors seem to have been addressed adequately at the time, or seen together as a worrying whole.

Shirley was admitted to hospital on 4 April 1982 with a head injury (ostensibly related to having fallen out of a cot onto her head) and 50 bruises on her body. Her brother, when examined, also had extensive bruising. Shirley was in this placement for just over four months, but was not seen by a social worker for a two-month period during that time.

Shirley's foster mother complained of headaches while the children were placed with the foster family, and visited her doctor on four separate occasions. Reder, Duncan and Gray note the importance of this sort of information.

> *Some parents gave hints in a disguised way that abuse was escalating, so that the practitioner first needed to translate the information in order to become aware of its significance . . . In the weeks preceding Shirley Woodcock's death, her foster mother repeatedly told the childminder and general practitioner about her severe headaches.*

> (Reder *et al.*, 1993, p91)

The report noted that assessments of foster carers only ever give a prognosis regarding their future capacity and abilities to care for children in public care. *At the point of approval, new foster parents are untried and untested. Thereafter, it must never be taken for granted that simply because they are approved as foster parents, they will always be able to cope* (Hammersmith and Fulham, 1984, p25). The first review of a foster carer and subsequent reviews offer opportunities to evaluate a foster carer's abilities to 'cope', and to test out the prognosis reached in the assessment report.

Derbyshire and Nottinghamshire

On 4 December 1989 Janet Jones, a foster carer, received four concurrent prison sentences, including a life sentence, for the manslaughter and indecent assault of GS, a nine-month-old baby, and the wilful ill treatment and grievous bodily harm to SH, a toddler.

Mr and Mrs Jones lived in Nottinghamshire, and were approved as foster carers for Derbyshire County Council. Mrs Jones had a history of depression, but this did not come to light in her medical report for the fostering panel approval process. SH, a 16-month-old boy, was placed with them from 1 April 1980 to 2 August 1981. In August 1980 SH sustained a burn injury to his hand, for which Mrs Jones sought hospital treatment. She later commented to a social worker that SH *seemed to feel no pain* (Derbyshire and Nottinghamshire, 1990, p14). On 6 January 1981 Mrs Jones phoned SH's social worker saying that SH needed to go to hospital as he had lacerated his penis. These injuries were so serious that he subsequently needed three operations. The explanation for the injuries was that having just used the potty he caught his penis in a pushchair mechanism. This explanation, like Mrs Jones' explanation for the burn, was accepted without an investigation and no link was made, at the time, with his previous injury. On 15 January his social worker told SH's mother that: *as far as I was concerned I had no complaints about the Joneses and I would not consider moving him* (Derbyshire and Nottinghamshire, 1990, p17).

During SH's time with the Jones family, Benjamin G was placed with them on 12 March 1981 when he was under two months old. He had a serious congenital heart disease and died a week later on 19 March 1981.

During Benjamin G's short placement, Karen, Mr and Mrs Jones' adolescent daughter, was admitted to an adolescent psychiatric unit on 16 March 1981, returning home on 24 March 1981. During her stay she disclosed to the unit staff that her parents' relationship was poor, and that she was afraid to leave her mother alone with SH. She said that she had seen her mother bang SH's head on the floor, and force food down his throat. This was relayed by the psychiatric unit by phone to the social services department (SSD). This referral was complicated by the unit staff saying that the information was confidential. SH's social worker, having received this information, wrote in the file: *decided not to remove SH on this information as it may be inaccurate, fantasy or part of K's illness* (Derbyshire and Nottinghamshire, 1990, p20). No link was made to SH's previous injuries.

In June 1981 a new social worker was allocated to SH's case. In the previous social worker's transfer summary there was no mention of the burn to SH's hand or to the injuries to his penis. On 2 August 1981 SH was returned 'home on trial'. Despite the social worker's seeming failure to identify a worrying pattern of injuries to SH, or to follow up the unit's telephone conversation regarding Karen's concerns about her mother's care of SH, the SSD Area Officer did have concerns. A decision was therefore made that no further placements should be made with the Jones family, while they had a six-month break from fostering, and work was done with them. Their own daughter's admission to an adolescent psychiatric unit would have been reason alone for this decision to have been made. The inquiry report noted the lack of fostering panel minutes recording the decision-making processes involved with this foster family. The Area Officer was recorded to have thought that Mrs Jones was psychologically ill, and that he was worried by SH's accidents. At this point, the Jones' first period as approved foster carers ended.

Mr and Mrs Jones were re-approved by the same council in June 1984. There was no information sought from the adolescent psychiatric unit during this 1984 assessment, and no references were taken up. During the reassessment Mr and Mrs Jones said that all previous family difficulties were resolved. Commenting on this assessment the inquiry team noted: *There were many serious errors and omissions. A contributory cause of them seemed to be a basic disbelief that foster parents could harm a child, coupled with inadequate assessment practices* (Derbyshire and Nottinghamshire, 1990, p45).

The family fostered a number of children short term between July 1984 and 10 April 1988. GS, a baby girl, was placed with the Joneses on 29 June 1988. She was just over two months old at the time. The plan was that the placement would last for about three months while an assessment was undertaken with her mother, to ascertain whether or not she was able to care for GS. If returning to her mother proved impossible GS would be placed with an adoptive family. GS was described as being passive with food, and there were concerns regarding her poor weight gain. On one occasion she was found by the hospital to have a urine infection. During this placement Mrs Jones cancelled or changed a number of adoption medical appointments for GS, as well as GS's medical appointments set up to monitor her weight.

By December 1988 prospective adoptive parents were being considered. They visited the Jones' home on 2 December 1988 and reported that they had found lumps behind GS's ears, and that they thought she seemed small. Mrs Jones later reported that she had taken

GS to see the GP and that the lumps behind GS's ears were thought, by the doctor, to be swollen glands. On 5 January 1989 GS's social worker received a phone call from Mrs Jones to say that they had had a difficult Christmas because of family members having colds, and that she did not want to take GS to see the dietician on 6 January as planned. However, Mrs Jones did go to the hospital for the appointment with GS and GS's social worker but said that GS should not have her clothes removed to be weighed, because of her cold. Both the social worker and the dietician agreed. They were to be seen at the hospital again on 11 January. On 8 January a member of the fostering team visited Mrs Jones who said that she wanted GS moved as she was so tired; indeed she wanted to give up fostering altogether. The social worker said that on that visit she *noticed GS give Mrs Jones a strange look* (Derbyshire and Nottinghamshire, 1990, p60).

The day before the next hospital appointment, to monitor GS's weight, Mrs Jones phoned GS's social worker to say that the appointment would have to be changed as they were going away. The appointment was changed first to 20 January and then to 25 January. At this point a hospital doctor intervened saying that this prospective appointment was too far away, and that GS should be seen at the hospital on 20 January. It later transpired that Mrs Jones was not away with her husband, but rather he had taken time off to work at home. On 18 January GS was taken by ambulance to hospital where she died the following day. She had a fracture to the skull, from which she died, and injuries to her vagina and anus and bruising to her buttocks that were inflicted about 10–14 days earlier. She also had a healed fracture of her right clavicle.

The inquiry report noted that GS was seen, either at home or at the hospital, 17 times between 29 June 1988 and 6 January 1989. The first foster carer review undertaken with the family was in 1985. The report notes that *where there were feedback forms on placements for the foster parent annual reviews no adverse comment was made and the Joneses continued to impress as a capable and caring family* (Derbyshire and Nottinghamshire, 1990, p64). The inquiry report concluded that the previous concerns from their first period of fostering were not sufficiently held in mind. If they had been then the pattern of wanting to change medical appointments might have been addressed.

The inquiry report made 59 recommendations. Recommendation 15.6 noted that all injuries to children in foster parents' homes should be recorded on the foster parents' file. Recommendation 18.59 states that *Prospective foster parents who apply for approval outside their local authority area should, as a precautionary measure, be asked their reasons for so doing* (Derbyshire and Nottinghamshire, 1990, p107). The report importantly tried to tackle the complexity of the working relationship between SSWs and foster carers:

> *The relationship between social workers and foster carers is difficult and demanding. The foster carer is required to be frank in every aspect of their lives, and the social worker has to build an atmosphere of trust where there is no inhibition on discussion of either success or failure. When trust has been established it may be necessary to use the information given because of that relationship in ways which the carer will see as hurtful.*

> (Derbyshire and Nottinghamshire, 1990, p85)

The focus of the SSW always has to be on the foster child, and cannot be diverted by misinterpretation of the SSW's role, as just being a support person for the foster carer. Supervision and support have to go hand in hand, the foster child being the centre of attention of both.

Wakefield

In 2007 the Wakefield Inquiry (Parrott *et al.*, 2007) examined the circumstances surrounding two male foster carers' (IW and CF) sexual abuse of foster children in their care. They were approved by Wakefield Council in July 2003, as short-term foster carers, but were given prison sentences in June 2006 for the sexual abuse of four boys, whom they had fostered.

IW and CF fostered 18 children during their relatively short fostering career. The inquiry team concluded that the assessment of them as prospective foster carers had insufficiently considered significant psycho-social aspects of them as individuals, and importantly of them as a couple. The inquiry report noted the inadequate supervision of the social worker involved, and the lack of rigorous scrutiny regarding allegations that were made about the foster carers. Like Munro (2011) the authors of the report concluded that procedurally driven practice, which in this case didn't even comply fully with the existing procedures, was problematic. They wrote: *The work has become more process-driven with less emphasis on individualised relationship-based practice and the use of discretion* (Parrott *et al.*, 2007, p151).

Laird notes that they were inexperienced foster carers who had many troubled children placed with them, as a result of Wakefield Council's shortage of foster carers.

> *Many of the children placed with CF and IW had previously been sexually abused and exhibited sexualised and challenging behaviour . . . Any one of these children would have presented considerable challenges in terms of their care even for the most experienced of foster carers. Yet, during the one-and-a-half year period from July 2003 to January 2005 these newly approved foster carers were to look after 18 different children each with substantial and complex needs.*
>
> (Laird, 2010, pp195–6)

The inquiry report noted that some social workers involved with the case seemed to have been preoccupied with the carers' sexual orientation, and with not wanting to appear to negatively discriminate against them as gay men:

> *. . . alongside anxieties on their part about being or being seen as prejudiced against gay people. The fear of being discriminatory led them to fail to discriminate between the appropriate and the abusive. Discrimination based on prejudice is not acceptable, especially not in social work or any public service. Discrimination founded on a professional judgement on a presenting issue, based on knowledge, assessed evidence and interpretation, is at the heart of good social work practice. These anxieties about discrimination have deep roots, we argue – in social work training, professional identity and organisational cultures . . .*
>
> (Parrott *et al.*, 2007, p164)

On the same point Brown and Cocker comment:

> *This report was a sharp reminder for social workers that alongside the need to make sure that practice and service delivery should never negatively discriminate against people on the grounds of gender, sexuality, age, race, religion and disability (as indeed is required by law in the UK under the Equality Act 2006), social workers also have a professional duty not to lose sight of the need to analyse and synthesise material to form professional judgments. Discrimination in its correct non prejudicial form is an essential ingredient in this analysis and synthesis in social work practice.*

> (Brown and Cocker, 2011, pp137–8)

Like the Gloucestershire report regarding Mrs Spry below (Gloucestershire Safeguarding Children Board, 2008) the Wakefield Inquiry recorded the power of CF and IW to manipulate the system that was there to supervise, monitor and support them. Related to a particular incident, and their SSW's failure to challenge the foster carers, the report noted: *This significant breach of their boundaries as foster carers was not addressed and challenged, once again signalling to CF and IW that they could be successful in bullying and manipulating the system to get what they wanted* (Parrott *et al.*, 2007, p88).

In 2004 the Commission for Social Care Inspection noted that Wakefield Council's annual foster carer reviews *had not always been undertaken, and where they had, these were not brought back to panel. This is a regulatory failing which needs addressing . . .* (Parrott *et al.*, 2007, p30). The opportunity for the review of the foster carers to act as a vehicle to properly scrutinise the quality of the foster care being offered, as well as the effectiveness of the supervision and support being afforded the foster carers, was lost in this case. IW and CF's first annual review on 6 July 2004 was deferred halfway through and re-convened on 14 September 2004. The review meeting was halted by the reviewing officer (RO) because material came to light that he had not had the opportunity to consider. In line with Wakefield Council's own procedures, prior to the review meeting, the RO would have expected to have had copies of written contributions from the foster carers, the SSW and the social workers for each of the children placed with IW and CF since their approval, as well as their most recent health report. Not all these documents were made available by the 6 July review meeting.

The inquiry team concluded that the SSW had written the foster carers' contribution for them for the 14 September review, and surmised that because the foster carers had not done their review paperwork the SSW covered for this. The inquiry team thought that in part this was related to IW and CF's bullying relationship with their SSW, and her resulting inability to challenge them. The report comments on the poor quality of the SSW's paperwork presented to the 14 September review, as follows: there were inaccuracies in the record of children placed with the foster carers since their approval; there was no record of foster children's views about their placements with CF and IW; there was no record of training that the foster carers had attended since their approval; and the SSW's report was described as a *rambling unstructured narrative* (Parrott *et al.*, 2007, p90).

The review paperwork had not been checked and signed off by the SSW's manager prior to it being sent to the RO. The RO took weeks before his report from the 14 September review meeting was submitted to the fostering team. The inquiry team concluded that *decision-making and management oversight in relation to this annual review was poor* (Parrott *et al.*, 2007, p82).

At the end of the foreshortened 6 July review the RO recommended that, despite worrying matters outlined in both the social worker for a foster child's report, and a birth parent's letter of complaint about the foster carers, CF and IW should continue to be approved as foster carers and have children placed with them. The inquiry team thought that the RO should have recommended, to the fostering panel, that their approval as foster carers remain in place but that no children be placed with them while matters were further investigated before the reconvened September review.

Commenting on the RO's role in the review meeting of 14 September the report criticises his lack of rigour and effectiveness and reads as follows:

> There is no evidence that IRO challenged or queried the statements or lack of key information in FCW2's report, or that he competently undertook the role of the review chair in facilitating analysis and weighing up information before arriving at conclusions.

> (Parrott *et al.*, 2007, p92)

Recommendation 27 of the inquiry report suggested foster carers' first reviews, after their approval, be conducted earlier than the statutory minimum of a year. Unfortunately, this recommendation was ignored by the Department of Education in the revision of the Fostering Service Regulations in 2011 (Department of Education, 2011b).

> The experience of this case emphasises strongly the value of early reviews of all newly approved foster carers, much earlier than the current statutory requirement . . . It is not appropriate that any potentially damaging and abusive foster carers should be without a review for 12 months.

> (Parrott *et al.*, 2007, p141)

The inquiry team made 41 recommendations, as well as summarising research and knowledge available at the time, relevant to the case. This inquiry report remains the most detailed case study of foster care that we have in the UK.

Mrs Spry

Mrs Spry was an adopter, a local authority foster carer and a private foster carer during the 20 years that she cared for other people's children. She started to foster in 1984, but her caring career was abruptly ended in December 2004 when a young person who had recently left her care disclosed serious abuse. Mrs Spry had originally privately fostered a sibling group of five. She had been a local authority foster carer from 1985 to 1994. By 1994 she had secured Orders for each of the children placed with her, and was therefore no longer a local authority foster carer. From 1994 she removed the children from their schools and home educated them.

At various points in Mrs Spry's fostering and adoption career concerns were raised, for example, when she was being assessed to adopt the two oldest girls. Each time concerns were raised, the fact that the children had already been living with her for some time, and their need for stability and continuity, took precedence over concerns some professionals expressed about the quality of her childcare. The SCR report noted that between 1990 and 2000 there were concerns raised regarding Mrs Spry's care of the children on 12 separate occasions. *However, the referrals seem to have been seen in isolation, with no correlation of the referrals or identification of a concerning pattern of care which was emerging* (Gloucestershire Safeguarding Children Board, 2008, p6).

Tragically, in September 2000, Mrs Spry's 37-year-old birth daughter and one of the five siblings placed with her (aged 16) were killed in a car accident. Two of the other children placed with her were also injured, one seriously. The seriously injured young person was aged 14 at the time. She had to have a number of operations as a result of the accident, and because of her injuries used a wheelchair until she finally left the placement. The inference in the SCR report was that she kept using the wheelchair longer than was necessary.

In December 2004 the two remaining children placed with Mrs Spry were removed after their sister disclosed the abuse she had experienced. The four young people's disclosures included emotional, physical and sexual abuse and neglect. They had been living in *squalor, with little in the way of comforts* (*London Evening Standard*, 2007). When Mrs Spry was tried, Bristol Crown Court heard that the children had been subjected to a *horrifying catalogue of cruel and sadistic treatment* (*London Evening Standard*, 2007).

There are a number of striking features in this case. The report notes that Mrs Spry had been assessed as to her capacity to care for children as a foster carer, and again as an adopter. Although some concerns were raised during the adoption assessment the report notes that:

> *Mrs Spry's application to be a foster parent, and then an adoptive parent, eventually went through without any strong challenges or dissent. Concerns were noted about Mrs Spry's abilities as a parent at times, but, on balance, it was felt to be in the children's interest to remain with Mrs Spry and to have legal security of placement with her. The placements outwardly appeared to be satisfactorily meeting the children's needs. There is some suggestion that Mrs Spry's dominant personality was allowed to drive relationships with statutory agencies.*

> (Gloucestershire Safeguarding Children Board, 2008, p4)

Mrs Spry was a Jehovah's Witness and although the report does not suggest there is a link between her religion and her abuse of the children, it infers that her religion might have clouded professionals' views about Mrs Spry's parenting style, as well as her lifestyle. In other words, social workers might have associated some of her behaviour, quite wrongly, with her religion and have felt anxious about challenging her for fear of seeming negatively discriminatory. Similar dynamics were explored in the Wakefield Inquiry above, not relating to religion but rather to sexuality and sexual orientation (Parrott *et al.*, 2007). The

Gloucestershire report emphasised the importance of professionals not accepting poor parenting whatever the reason. Recommendation 14 states:

The impact on the lifestyle of children who are cared for by parents or carers, who display eccentric, unusual or rigid styles of parenting, should be thoroughly assessed. Child protection training should emphasise that eccentric or unusual parenting must not be used as a reason to accept or excuse unacceptable levels of childcare.

(Gloucestershire Safeguarding Children Board, 2008, p9)

Similar to the findings of the Wakefield Inquiry, Mrs Spry was seen as a controlling person and Children *difficult to engage in professional interventions* (Gloucestershire Safeguarding Children Board, p3). Mrs Spry seemed to contrive to make sure that the children were not seen independently, so their voices were not heard. This case highlighted the importance of health, education and social services professionals working closely together. The second oldest girl's school raised concerns regarding her being over punished and Mrs Spry exhibiting a lack of warmth towards her. Indeed, social services put in place an assessment of this child's care, but as Mrs Spry would not co-operate the assessment was not completed. The court subsequently made the Adoption Order with this assessment still incomplete. Mrs Spry had a lot of contact with medical professionals claiming that the children had physical, emotional and behavioural problems. Indeed, three of the children were prescribed Ritalin. The whole picture of the quality of the care for these children was lost as the various parts of the multi-professional jigsaw remained dislocated.

Child V and Mr and Mrs A

Child V was placed with Mr and Mrs A from a hospital special care baby unit by Rotherham Metropolitan Council. She had been treated for neonatal abstinence syndrome as a result of her mother's heroin use during pregnancy. On 7 January 2007 Child V died in hospital from a heart attack and multiple organ failure. She was found to have 13 fractured ribs, which were believed to have been broken about four weeks prior to her death, and there was evidence of a more recent re-fracture to one rib. Child V also had tears to her top and bottom lip frenuli, and extensive nappy rash. These injuries were believed, by Rotherham Safeguarding Children Board, to have been inflicted in the foster home. The police carried out an investigation but no charges were brought.

Mr and Mrs A were approved as short-term foster carers in June 2005. The SCR report records that a foster carer review report was submitted to the fostering panel, but no review meeting had been conducted with the foster carers. The report notes that the fostering service *was under strain and struggling to meet its statutory obligations* (Rotherham Safeguarding Children Board, 2009, p5).

There were four concerning matters about these foster carers' care of children during their fostering career between June 2005 and January 2007, in addition to the serious injuries to Child V. The council's inability to see patterns emerging about these carers' fostering practice and direct care of children was evident. Like the Mrs Spry and

Derbyshire and Nottinghamshire cases each worrying incident was dealt with in isolation. The report comments on some concerns related to their own birth children: their daughter's weight loss, and their son's and foster children's missed medical appointments. In addition the limited growth of four foster children they cared for was not identified as significant.

The SSW visited the foster family in the 51 days that Child V was with Mr and Mrs A on one occasion. This was pertinent as the fostering manager had gone against the fostering panel's recommendation, and the ADM's decision that another baby should not be placed with them at the time Child V was placed. The report concluded that *there had been a lack of critical analysis of the assessment of the foster carers and their care, made worse by the inadequate level of supervision and review* (Rotherham Safeguarding Children Board, 2009, p8).

The assessment of them as prospective foster carers did not address the fact that Mr A worked nights, which in this case meant that in effect Mrs A was a single foster carer. The SCR report argued that there needed to be more independent scrutiny of foster carers, and that the relationship developed between foster carer and SSW should not inhibit investigations. Concerning incidents were not looked at in the whole; rather each one was dealt with as a discrete matter, which led to a failure to identify worrying patterns. The Safeguarding Board recommended that all recommendations for training made from foster carer reviews should include timeframe requirements.

Mr and Mrs B

Mr and Mrs B were foster carers for Rotherham Metropolitan Council. In June 2008 Mr B was sentenced to 12 years' imprisonment for sexual offences against three foster children in his and his wife's care. They were approved as foster carers in June 1998, and had 13 children placed with them between 1998 and 2008. They had three adult children of their own and four grandchildren. None of their children were interviewed as part of their assessment as prospective foster carers.

The Safeguarding Children Board uncovered Mr B's history of alcohol misuse, which was unbeknown to the fostering panel, as well as evidence of domestic violence, which, however, was not verified. At the start of their fostering career Mr B was the main carer as Mrs B worked. This changed when Mrs B left her job, and Mr and Mrs B both became full-time foster carers. They had health problems but were never re-assessed because of this. Mr B had an oppressive parenting style and the Board's report revealed that children in their care were not interviewed separately from their foster carers. Mr B attended training and indeed became a foster carer trainer himself.

The level of supervision from an allocated SSW was apparently inconsistent and, regarding their foster carer reviews, the SCR report observed that: *although fostering reviews took place, they did not happen annually, as required by Regulations, and it is not clear what information was presented to the fostering panel following each review* (Rotherham Safeguarding Children Board, 2010, p3). Importantly the foster children were not seen separately, away from their foster carers, so their independent voices were not heard.

Learning from inquiry and SCR reports

These seven reports have findings and recommendations relevant to social work and foster care. I have grouped these under the headings of: the regulatory framework; the assessment process; inter-professional communication; resources; and skills acquisition or application. The headings are drawn from Reder and Duncan (2004), as noted earlier, and used flexibly. For example, under 'inter-professional communication' I have included communication between local authorities, as well as between social workers within different teams in the same local authority, and added the regulatory framework.

The regulatory framework

In all the above cases there were breaches of Regulations. The Dennis O'Neill report (Home Office, 1945) stated that Regulations have to be followed to the letter, but that they should be treated as a minimum, not a maximum, requirement. The Rotherham Safeguarding Children Board (2010) report records how 65 years later Regulations were still not being met. The Department of Health, in its review of inquiry reports of the 1980s, notes, in respect to fostering, that the then Regulations *prescribe only minimum Standards to safeguard a vulnerable group of children, but even these minimum Standards were neglected and some in places seemed unknown* (1991, p97).

It is important to heed a cautionary note when looking at inquiry reports and SCRs, which are in effect case studies. A limitation of looking at only these inquiry and SCR reports is that, in so doing, we do not consider other cases where regulatory requirements were not met, but nothing untoward resulted. In other words, non-compliance with Regulations does not automatically equate to child injury or death, even though non-compliance was a consistent variable in these cases. The non-compliance with regulatory requirements, in these seven cases, sat alongside a number of other variables that, combined, conspired to create a lack of rigorous assessment and effective supervision of the foster carers.

The assessment process

The assessment process of prospective foster carers is primarily about assessing their suitability to become foster carers, but it is also about identifying a person's or couple's strengths, and areas that require further development. The period during which the assessment is undertaken is the time when the fostering service and the assessor establish a relationship with the foster carer. At its most basic, the assessment should screen out people who are not suitable to become foster carers. This screening process variously involves: checks required through Regulation; gathering references; the self-evaluation by the foster carer; and the assessment and evaluation by the assessor. The assessor's assessment and evaluation requires a sophisticated ability to establish a trusting, empathetic, facilitative relationship that enables rigorous and probing assessment and evaluation.

The above inquiry and SCR reports note deficits in the quality of the assessment of the foster carers. These deficits involved failures in two regards. First, the failure to collect and evaluate available information; for example, through gathering information from

Belfast Metropolitan Colleg
Millfield LRC

the police, or from medical records. Second, poor assessment skills in both eliciting and analysing information that became known, or addressing dynamics that became apparent, during the assessment process. The first included crucial information about the applicants not being gathered including: previous domestic violence (Dennis O'Neill and Mr and Mrs B), depression (Derbyshire and Nottingham) and alcohol misuse (Mr and Mrs B). More complex matters in the second included the lack of explicit assessment of psycho-social areas for the individuals involved and the couple's relationship (Wakefield Inquiry); and the lack of addressing key practical areas such as the implications of one person within a couple working night shifts (Child V and Mr and Mrs A).

Assessment is not a one-off event, but rather is an ongoing process. Reviews of foster carers act as reassessments, enabling reconsideration of their suitability to continue to be approved as foster carers, and the evaluation of the quality of the foster care they provide. The inquiry and SCR reports above note the lost review opportunities that could have helped those involved identify worrying patterns. This is most explicitly addressed in the Wakefield Inquiry report.

Supervision of the assessor was discussed in a number of the above reports, as an important and necessary ingredient to make possible the thorough assessment of prospective foster carers. Monkton put it quite simply as the need to have more than one person's view as to the suitability of a person or people becoming foster carers (Home Office, 1945).

Inter-professional communication

Effective inter-professional communication has to be imbedded in social work and foster care practice to enable a holistic assessment to be made of the foster carer, the foster child and the quality of foster care being afforded that child. Holistic work requires excellent multi-professional and inter-professional work, and good communication within local authorities, between their component parts, between local authorities and independent fostering agencies (where a foster child is placed with an IFA foster carer) and crucially between children looked after teams and fostering teams.

In a number of the above cases there was evidence of poor working relationships between the foster child's social worker and the foster carer's SSW, which was associated with entrenched positions being taken by the different parties involved, about what was best for a foster child. This 'splitting' dynamic was apparent in the Shirley Woodcock Inquiry, the Derbyshire and Nottinghamshire Inquiry and the Wakefield Inquiry. I look at the working relationship between the SSW and the foster child's social worker in Chapter 5 as it is, in my view, central to enabling successful foster care, and is crucial when allegations, complaints or concerns against foster carers are being investigated.

Understanding the circumstances of a foster carer, their household and a foster child's experience within that foster placement necessitates the sharing of information between all professionals working with the foster carer, and the foster child. Yet, it is not just the sharing of information that is imperative, but rather the ability to make sense of it, and identify its significance. For example, medical information in the Shirley Woodcock Inquiry, the Derbyshire and Nottinghamshire Inquiry, the Mrs Spry SCR, the Child V and Mr and Mrs A SCR and the Mr and Mrs B SCR reports all provided clues to difficult emerging patterns of behaviour, and poor outcomes for the foster children.

Reports from school and information regarding school attendance can be significant in identifying difficulties for school-age children. Withdrawal of foster children from school happened in both the Dennis O'Neill and the Mrs Spry cases. Both were indicative of the foster carers wanting less scrutiny of their foster children by the authorities.

The Dennis O'Neill Inquiry and the Derbyshire and Nottingham Inquiry reports identified the importance of local authorities working closely together, and the problems associated when bureaucratic wrangling takes precedence over the interests of foster children.

Resources

In all seven cases shortages of resources were noted. However, scarce resources would have been applicable to other cases in the local authorities concerned when these tragedies occurred. Similar to the point raised above, compliance with Regulations alone does not guarantee good outcomes, and neither do adequate resources. Most of the inquiry and SCR reports noted that pressure on resources might have contributed to the inadequate frequency of visits to the foster placements, which were not undertaken at the regulatory required level. Conversely, in the Derbyshire and Nottinghamshire case the family were seen by various professionals 17 times between 29 June 1988 and 6 January 1989, and the outcome was still the death of a foster child. The point here is that, of course the required level of visits should be made as a minimum, but it is the quality of the professional contact with the foster carer and foster child during those visits and the probing nature of them that is likely to make a difference. What is needed of SSWs' visits to foster carers is both quantity and quality, not quantity alone.

Skills acquisition or application

Some of the skills social workers need, as they apply to social work and foster care, include: organisational and administrative skills; observational skills; report writing skills; communication skills; and cognitive skills, including making judgements and decision making. The above inquiry and SCR reports identified a number of gaps in the skills of the social workers involved in the cases. In retrospect it is easy to identify social workers' skills deficits, but some of the social work dilemmas and the dynamics involved in these cases were complex. For example, the Shirley Woodcock Inquiry and the Mrs Spry SCR reports recorded the dilemma faced by social workers regarding whether it was better to move a child from a placement, thus causing disruption for them, or leave them in a concerning placement. In both cases the social workers involved made the wrong decisions, but the decisions were not necessarily straightforward, and were dependent on the partial information available to them at the time. Rather than looking at each concern about a foster carer, or incident, or injury to a child in isolation, what might have improved professional judgements and decision making would have been the identification of gaps in information, and patterns of concerning matters. This opportunity was lost in most of the cases above.

Identifying patterns, when a social worker assesses prospective foster carers, or when they are supervising foster carers, is partly enabled through the social worker's own supervision. As noted above, the foster carer and SSW's relationship is a complex one and has the potential to become unknowingly collusive. Thus, the quality of supervision the SSW receives is important in addressing this collusive potential.

The importance of observation can be identified in the above reports. Le Riche and Tanner cover the knowledge and skills of observation, as applied to social work practice, and their book is valuable for those working in foster care (Le Riche and Tanner, 1998). When Mrs Edwards visited Bank Farm on 20 December 1944 she knew that Dennis O'Neill's placement with the Goughs was not satisfactory. She observed how Dennis looked, his manner and Mr and Mrs Gough's demeanour towards the children. She was not told about these things, she observed them. The Derbyshire and Nottingham report noted that the worker on her visit to Mrs Jones on 8 January 1989 observed GS giving Mrs Jones 'a strange look'. If this 'look' had been explored GS's circumstances might have been further investigated.

In a number of the above cases the voice of the child was either insufficiently heard, or not heard at all. In some of the cases foster children were not interviewed separately from their foster carers, meaning that they were unlikely to feel in a position to say what they really thought or felt. In the Derbyshire and Nottinghamshire case it was the foster carers' daughter who tried to alert the authorities to her mother's abuse of a foster child. She was not taken seriously because at the time she was an in-patient in an adolescent psychiatric unit, so what she said appears to have been misinterpreted as being part of her illness, and consequently dismissed. In the Wakefield Inquiry it became evident that a parent of one of the foster children tried to raise the alarm, but again her views were given insufficient weight. Sometimes parents of foster children do make false allegations against foster carers, and it does not take a lot of empathy or intelligence to understand why. They might, for example, be in care proceedings fighting to have their child back, and as a result make an allegation against a foster carer to try to undermine their child's placement. Birth parents can feel they have little or no influence, and making allegations against foster carers can be a potentially powerful intervention. On the other hand, birth parents might be alerting social workers to matters of real importance about the quality of the foster care to which their child is being subjected. All complaints and allegations have to be explored properly, irrespective of whom the complainant or alleger is, because they might have foundation, as they did in the Wakefield and Derbyshire and Nottinghamshire cases. Foster children, foster carers' children and birth parents all need to be heard, as of course do foster carers. In the Shirley Woodcock and Derbyshire and Nottinghamshire cases the foster carers said that they were not coping, but the seriousness of what they were trying to convey was neither heard nor understood.

The quality of social workers' reports was commented upon in the Wakefield Inquiry report, as was the importance of the accuracy of the content of reports. The significance of the full facts of a case being absent in transfer summaries was noted in the Derbyshire and Nottinghamshire Inquiry report. The full facts being recorded in transfer or closing summaries is particularly pertinent when a foster carer moves from one fostering service to another or when, as in the Derbyshire and Nottinghamshire case, they have two separate episodes of being approved as foster carers by the same fostering service. It is essential that SSWs and their supervisors are conversant with a foster carer's history and the detail of their foster care career.

Mr and Mrs B's and Mrs Spry's SCRs and the Wakefield Inquiry report all raise the issue of working with powerful foster carers who manage to create bullying and evasive dynamics between themselves and other professionals responsible for the children for whom they are caring. The Mrs Spry and the Mr and Mrs B cases also raised the issue of SSWs needing to directly address parenting styles, to make sure that those styles are conducive to foster children's happiness and development. The Wakefield Inquiry and Mrs Spry's SCR cover the thorny and complex area of social workers feeling anxious about challenging foster carers when they think they might be accused of being negatively discriminatory; in Mrs Spry's case because of her religion, and in the Wakefield case because of the foster carers being gay. SSWs need the confidence to make sure that their supervision of foster carers is always child-focused. To have this confidence necessitates having the support of their manager and fostering service, to ensure they can be resilient in the face of manipulative, evasive and bullying dynamics (Laird, 2013). Working with difficult dynamics, addressing parenting styles and working in an inclusive yet rigorous manner are about the minutiae of what takes place between SSWs and foster carers. They are complex areas of social work practice impacting upon the quality of social work undertaken with foster carers, and require social workers to have the requisite inter-personal communication and intervention knowledge and skills to work capably, overseen by a trusting, yet probing, supervisory relationship with their manager.

Chapter summary

- This chapter focused on seven tragic sets of circumstances that led to either the death, or the abuse, of children in foster care.

- Although these situations are rarities, the related reports act as case studies to enable better understanding of how and why sometimes things go very wrong.

- Heywood, writing about the death of Dennis O'Neill, noted the public reaction to the realisation that children are sometimes harmed in foster care. *The public disquiet was profound. That a child, removed from his own home because of its bad conditions and entrusted for his greater good, to the public care, should yet experience even worse neglect and cruelty leading directly to his death* . . . was deeply shocking (1965, p142).

- When children are removed from their own families and placed in foster care, the bare minimum expected is that they are safeguarded from harm.

- Rigorous assessment and supervision of foster carers can enable children to develop their potential in foster care, and ensure they are safe. Both entail effective multi-professional work.

- Because of fostering services' responsibilities to foster children it is crucial that we learn from these reports' findings and recommendations. Writing over 65 years ago Sir Monkton's words are still as pertinent now as they were then, reminding social work practitioners and fostering services that Regulations have to be followed to the letter, but must only ever be seen as a minimum requirement not a maximum attainment (Home Office, 1945).

- The quality of the social work undertaken with foster carers can make a difference to outcomes for foster children.

FURTHER READING

Biehal, N and Parry, E (2010) *Maltreatment and Allegations of Maltreatment in Foster Care: A Review of the Evidence.* York: The University of York Social Policy Research Unit/London: The Fostering Network.

This literature review gives a good grounding in the knowledge available relating to foster care and the maltreatment of foster children.

Parrott, B, MacIver, A and Thoburn, J (2007) *Independent Inquiry Report into the Circumstances of Child Sexual Abuse by Two Foster Carers in Wakefield.* Wakefield: Wakefield County Council.

This inquiry report is one of the most illuminating case studies we have about the detail of the interface between foster care and social work.

Chapter 4

Assessment of prospective foster carers

CHAPTER OBJECTIVES

By the end of this chapter, readers should:

- be familiar with the necessary content and process of the assessment of foster carers;
- understand how theory and research can help inform this complex area of social work practice;
- have an awareness of how our own assessment practice can be fine-tuned to make sure that we offer a facilitative, rigorous assessment to prospective foster carers who, if approved, will in turn offer foster children the high-quality care they should experience.

Introduction

The assessment of prospective foster carers is a pivotal process for fostering services and those wanting to become foster carers. It is the moment when the fostering service's necessity to recruit, assess and approve capable foster carers comes into contact with the hopes, fears and aspirations of individuals applying to be foster carers. There is considerable pressure on fostering services to recruit, assess and approve foster carers, because there continues to be a shortage of fostering households required for the number of placements needed for children who are looked after, and to meet their diverse needs. Robert Tapsfield, Chief Executive of the Fostering Network, in May 2013 stated that we *need to recruit 9,000 more foster carers this year alone, particularly for teenagers, sibling groups and disabled children* (Tapsfield, 2013).

This chapter covers

- Recruitment of foster carers
- Types of foster care
- Assessment in general

- Assessment of foster carers in particular

- What the Standards, Guidance and Regulations say

- What needs to be considered in all foster carer assessments

- Tools for undertaking assessments

- Assessing sameness and difference

- Recruiting and assessing particular groups of foster carers

- Ethnicity, nationality and religion

- The assessment of lesbian and gay prospective foster carers.

Recruitment

On 31 March 2012, 75 per cent (50,260) of children looked after by local authorities were living with foster carers (BAAF, 2013a). This number has steadily grown in the UK since the 1940s and, as Thomas and Philpot note, *in the past 30 years fostering has shifted gear, both in the kinds of children and young people with whom it is concerned and also in the gradual professionalisation of its service* (2009, p13). This 'shift in gear' regarding the number of foster placements that have to be found, and the range of placements necessary to meet foster children's varied needs, means that the recruitment and retention of foster carers is a key concern for fostering services. It is therefore important that we have some idea about people who apply to be foster carers, and what their motives are for applying, to enable recruitment strategies and campaigns to be targeted and potentially successful.

The seriousness of the need to improve the effectiveness of the recruitment of foster carers is demonstrated by the Government's £250,000 contract, awarded to the Fostering Network in May 2013, to improve knowledge about how to recruit and retain foster carers in England, and thus inform fostering services' strategies and practices (The Fostering Network, 2013).

We already know quite a lot about what works in recruitment, who fosters and why they foster, all of which comprise information to enable fostering services to understand how to better their recruitment strategies and target potential applicants. Three studies published in 2012 contributed knowledge about who fosters and why they foster. Peake and Townsend's study (2012), which had over 1,400 respondents, found a number of interesting findings to inform recruitment strategies as follows: although most people in the sample were interested in fostering from when they were between 30 and 40 years of age, most people were approved much later in life as foster carers, between the ages of 40 to 45. The older the applicant the quicker their decision was to become a foster carer. Eighty-four per cent of the sample had their own children. Prior to fostering only 12 per cent of the sample were not working full time or part time outside the home. Nearly 50 per cent were working full time and 25 per cent worked part time. Sixty-three per cent had worked or done volunteering with children. People in the study's sample were motivated to foster for the following reasons:

- *opportunity for children to be part of the family (86 per cent);*

- *good thing for them or their family to do (77 per cent);*

- *wanted to work with children (69 per cent);*

- *own past experience (36 per cent);*

- *their partner wanted to do it (35 per cent).*

Financial arrangements for fostering were a consideration in 40% of people's decision to foster. Almost half saw fostering as a way to work from home.

(Peake and Townsend, 2012, p9)

Sebba's (2012) international literature review, addressing people's motivation to become foster carers, identified three main findings: that contact with people who foster, as a child or as an adult, encourages people to foster; the most effective form of information about fostering is through direct contact with foster carers, although fact sheets can be helpful; and, lastly, contact with foster carers who have inadequate support can act as a deterrent for people wanting to become foster carers. The study also identified similar motivations to those identified in the Peake and Townsend (2012) study but in addition found that the efficiency of response from a fostering service, when a potential foster carer made contact, impacted upon whether or not they pursued their initial interest in applying.

McDermid *et al.*'s (2012) literature review overall reflected the findings of the above two studies. In addition, in terms of characteristics of foster carers they found that: most foster-ing households were composed of married heterosexual couples, and cohabiting couples were underrepresented; foster carers were likely to be employed outside the home; most foster carers were middle aged and few were 35 years or younger; black and minority ethnic group foster carers were underrepresented, when compared to the same groups in the children looked after population; male carers were underrepresented; most foster carers had no educational qualification and the next largest group were educated only to GCSE level; fewer foster carers had university degrees compared to the wider population (McDermid *et al.*, 2012, p5).

The motivation to foster for the McDermid *et al.* study's sample reflected the previous studies' findings: liking children; people's previous personal histories; knowing there was a need for foster carers; their family circumstances that fitted with fostering; to extend/create their family; their children growing up; and altruism (McDermid *et al.*, 2012, pp5–6). They also found that remuneration was a factor, enabling, as it does, people to foster, and that the better the remuneration the more successful was recruitment and retention. This study considered barriers to recruitment which included: lack of confidence and understanding on behalf of the potential applicant; worries about being assessed; concerns about being seen to profit from caring for children; anxiety that a child might return to their family; apprehension about allegations being made against them; mistrust of social workers; social care's poor public image; fears about placement breakdown and stress.

Scott and Duncan's (2013) research undertaken for the Department of Education examined motivation to foster as well as some of the barriers and triggers potential applicants experienced. Like previous research they found people were motivated to foster in order to help children and society, as well as for the benefit of themselves. Key barriers that potential applicants identified related to: worries about the assessment process; the possible difficulties of fostering itself; and the impact it might have on them and their families. The researchers identify a plan for the Department of Education, which includes targeting particular groups as potential applicants.

An earlier review of the research findings, looking at the recruitment of foster carers, conducted by the Social Care Institute for Excellence (2004), found that successful campaigns had the following characteristics, reflecting the findings from the above studies done some eight years later:

- good knowledge of local area;

- close collaboration with experienced carers;

- systems in place for following up enquiries;

- using the local media;

- ongoing recruitment drives – not just one-offs;

- use of foster carers' own networks.

(Social Care Institute for Excellence, 2004)

The same year, 2004, the Fostering Network produced their good practice guidance for the recruitment of foster carers (The Fostering Network, 2004), giving helpful advice to fostering services about every aspect of recruitment, much of which is as relevant today as it was in 2004, and is in line with the research findings from the 2012 and 2013 studies outlined above.

It would seem then that contact with foster carers who have positive messages to convey is likely to encourage those considering applying to a fostering service to be assessed as a prospective foster carer, and that an agency that is ready to respond warmly and efficiently to inquiries is more likely to keep the goodwill of potential applicants. Given there is currently an ageing foster carer population, not a problem in itself but a population that will eventually retire, the recruitment of under 35 year olds might be a productive focus for fostering services, as well as targeting the recruitment of black and ethnic minority foster carers, when they are underrepresented. Foster carers' own families and social networks are fruitful sources to explore for foster carer recruitment and those potential individuals, because they have been exposed to foster care and often have a realistic view of what fostering entails.

Social workers and managers responsible for the recruitment of foster carers could benefit from taking on board the above studies' findings and their messages for practice, to help inform their strategic thinking. Social workers involved in recruitment have to consider their role as ambassadors for their fostering service, and the importance of engaging in a public relations exercise with warmth, clarity and efficiency, to ensure that their approach will encourage potential foster carer applicants, rather than put them off.

Types of foster care

What are applicants being assessed to do? Foster care covers a whole range of practices, some of which are called by different names by different fostering services. I have listed them in alphabetical order, and these include:

- emergency and short-term foster care, where the expectation is that a child is only going to be placed with a foster carer for between one night and a few months;
- family and friends foster care, where a foster carer looks after a child with whom they already have a connection;
- multi-dimensional treatment foster care/intensive foster care, where a foster carer and the foster child placed with them are part of a multi-professional, social learning theory, multi-dimensional treatment programme;
- parent and child foster care (Adams and Dibben, 2011), where a parent and their baby or young child are placed with a foster carer, while an assessment is undertaken to enable plans to be made about whether or not that child should remain with their parent;
- permanent foster care, where the intention is that a child placed with a foster carer will remain with them until they reach adulthood;
- remand foster care, where an alleged young offender is placed with foster carers while they await trial or sentencing;
- respite foster care, where a child stays with a foster carer for short periods of time from another foster carer;
- short break foster care, where a foster carer provides brief, but regular, care for a child with a disability who normally lives with their family;
- support foster care (Brown, Fry and Howard, 2005), where a foster carer works with a local authority, and a child and their family (birth or adoptive family), to try to enable that child to remain within their family by offering regular, defined support either for part of a day, overnight or for short periods of time, thus enabling that child to remain with their family.

The first of these foster care categories, 'emergency and short-term fostering', still a much used term, is a misnomer because placements anticipated to be for a few nights or months often last for a year or years, or turn into permanent foster placements or adoptive placements.

This chapter does not consider each of these categories individually, as that is beyond what is possible within one chapter, but rather looks at assessment of foster carers as it applies to them all. The fostering Guidance and Regulations, as they relate to the assessment of foster carers (Chapter 2), do not differentiate between different types of foster care, but rather consider what is required of all assessments of prospective foster carers.

Assessment: general pointers

Social work is awash with books about assessment (Whittington, 2007; Beckett, 2010; Milner and O'Byrne, 2009; Martin, 2010; Parker and Bradley, 2010; Walker and Beckett, 2010; Aspinwall-Roberts, 2012, to name but a few), most of which focus on assessment as it relates to safeguarding of adults and children, or assessment of need, and falls within what Wilson, Ruch, Lymbery and Cooper define as *suitability assessments* (2011, p275). Assessment of prospective foster carers is different again. However, this general literature is, in many respects, useful in informing the assessment of prospective foster carers.

Although now dated, Coulshed and Orme's (2006) CORE skills of assessment still apply to this area of social work practice: communication, observation, reflection and evaluation, all of which are critically important in the assessment of prospective foster carers. I consider each in turn.

- The effectiveness of the *communication skills* of the assessor impacts on the quality of the assessment undertaken, because the personality and behaviour of the assessor influences the openness of the applicant being assessed and, as a result, the information that is elicited. What is said between the applicant and assessor, the exchange of information and exploration of a foster carer's life story, are important components of the material that informs the thinking and decision making of the assessor, informing their recommendation as to whether or not a foster carer should be approved.

- However, equally important is the assessor's ability to *observe* the applicant, the dynamics between the applicant and those they live with and the dynamic between the applicant and the assessor. The assessor is also making an informed judgement about an applicant's home as a suitable environment for hypothetical foster children. That informed judgement can only be achieved through observation, and making sense of that which is observed.

- Observation and *reflection* essentially go hand in hand; as Holland observes, social workers' presence impacts upon any situation or interaction, and has to be taken into account. She writes: *the assessor must retain a reflexive awareness of the impact of their own presence and their beliefs, experience, professional status and knowledge on the interaction* (2011, p162). To be able to link observation and reflection requires what in social work education used to be called, and unfortunately has become less fashionable of late, 'self-awareness'. Self-awareness, an understanding of self, your own history and your impact on others, is crucial in assessing the influence you, as the assessor, have on those being assessed, and the assessment process itself.

- *Evaluation* necessitates the ability to analyse and synthesise all the material gathered from what has been said and observed, as well as from the statutory checks, references and feedback from preparation training that an applicant has attended. It is this evaluation, the informed analysis and synthesis, that helps the assessor decide what they will be recommending.

As more fostering services make use of independent social workers, who are either self-employed or working for private independent social work agencies, it is important that we remind ourselves that assessment is not, and cannot be, a one-off event, but rather it is part of a process. It is the first formal, sustained interaction that an applicant has with the fostering service that is undertaking the assessment, or has commissioned the assessment to be done by a third party. Walker and Beckett write:

> *It is important to think of assessment as a process rather than a one-off event. There should be a seam-less transition from assessment to intervention in a circular process that includes the crucial elements of planning and reviewing. Once completed, the circle begins again at the assessment stage of the process and so on.*

(Walker and Beckett, 2010, p13)

Although not writing about foster carer assessment, what Walker and Beckett address reflects the processes involved in social work and foster care practice; the assessment itself, the regular cycle of foster carer supervision and foster carer reviews. In cases where an assessment has been undertaken by a third party, an assessor who is not part of the fostering service, the handover from that assessor to the SSW, in cases where the applicant has been approved as a foster carer, is important for continuity of relationships and the transfer of information.

The process of assessment, defined by Milner and O'Byrne, fits with what is required when an assessment of a prospective foster carer is undertaken, even though their 'process' is not specific to foster care, but rather to assessment of need or safeguarding. Their distilled points include: *preparing for the task; collecting data; applying professional knowledge (practice wisdom as well as theory) to seek analysis, understanding or interpretation of the data; making judgements; deciding and/ or recommending* (2009, p4). Making judgements that inform an assessor's eventual recommendation to a fostering panel is informed by the analysis and synthesis of all the data collected as noted above.

Prospective foster carer assessments

There is a scarcity of research findings that inform practitioners about the effectiveness of assessment of foster carers; indeed we know little about whether the assessment process in itself is effective in approving capable foster carers who will enable foster children to thrive in their care (Luke and Sebba, 2013). Practitioners are therefore reliant on what might be described as 'practice experience' or 'practice wisdom' literature to inform their assessment practice. Even within this genre of publications there is surprisingly little. In my view Beesley's (2010) publication on assessment of foster carers and adopters, although geared to assessment as it relates to those applicants wanting to care for a child permanently, is applicable to all prospective foster carer assessments. Beesley advocates the use of Smale and Tuson's (1993) 'exchange model' to be utilised in foster carer assessments in that the assessment should be a joint enterprise, with both the assessor and applicant working in partnership, and learning through the process. She argues that specific theoretical approaches to assessment can enrich and inform the assessment process, and cites: psychodynamic, ecological, competence-/task-centred and educative approaches as being of value in this context, as well as an understanding of family systems and risk assessment (2010, pp19–21).

Beesley's suggested theoretical underpinnings should enable the assessor to develop, through the assessment period, an understanding of: the foster carer's past and how it impacts on their present life and relationships and might impact on their future role as a foster carer; how the foster carer experiences their family of origin and their current family relationships, and how that might impact on their foster care; and how matters relating to the applicant's understanding of their own experience of attachment, transition and loss could impact on their ability to work effectively with foster children, foster children's families, the fostering service and other professionals working with foster children.

At the same time as considering, and exploring, all of the above the assessor has to maintain, over time, a structured focus on: what foster carers have to do emotionally and practically; what personal attributes they need, particularly in terms of emotional and intellectual capacity; and their practical circumstances, whether or not they will realistically be able to manage being a foster carer, as well as the rest of their and their family members' lives. For the assessor to conclude that the applicant will be capable of delivering good quality foster care to children, all these aspects have to be explored in depth.

The foster carer assessment is also a process of education and development, enabling the prospective foster carer to learn about: what being a foster carer involves; the fostering service's expectations of their foster carers; attachment, transition and loss, and how these impact on foster children; and foster care and multi-professional working – what it will mean to be a key member of the 'team around the child' responsible for the realisation of that foster child's care plan.

Fundamental to the assessment of potential foster carers is the assessment of risk. At its most basic level the assessment of foster carers has to identify, through required regulatory checks and the skills and analytic, reflective abilities of the assessor, whether or not the applicant poses a potential risk to foster children, either through actively maltreating them or through their inability to adequately meet their varied needs.

What the Standards, Guidance and Regulations say

The requirements of the assessment of prospective foster carers are set out in:

- The NMS Standard 13 (Department of Education, 2011a, pp28–9).

- The Children Act 1989 Guidance and Regulations Volume 2: Care Planning, Placement and Case Review Regulation 24 and 25 (HM Government, 2010) in relation to children placed temporarily with family and friends carers.

- The Children Act 1989 Guidance and Regulations Volume 4: Fostering Services (HM Government, 2011, pp43–5).

- The Fostering Services (England) Regulations, Regulation 27 (Department of Education, 2011b, pp15–16) and Schedule 3 (Department of Education, 2011b, p27).

- Assessment and Approval of Foster Carers: Amendments to the Children Act 1989 Guidance and Regulations, Volume 4: Fostering Services (Department of Education, 2013b).

It is important that every aspect of the assessment and all checks and references are complete, before a properly quality assured assessment report, about a prospective foster carer, is presented to a fostering panel.

The required content of the prospective foster carer assessment, by that I mean what has to be covered, is set out in the Fostering Guidance and Regulations (Department of Education, 2011b; HM Government, 2011; Department of Education, 2013b). The assessment of foster carers in England is a two-stage process: the first stage required by Regulation 26 (Department of Education, 2011b) includes gathering information regarding the following:

- obtain the information specified in Part 1 of Schedule 3:

  o the applicant's full name, address and date of birth;

  o details of the applicant's health, supported by a medical report;

  o particulars of other adult household members;

  o particulars of children in the applicant's family (whether or not they are members of the household) and any other children in the household;

  o particulars of the household's accommodation;

  o the outcome of any request or application made by the applicant, or any member of the applicant's household, to foster or adopt children or for registration as an early or later years provider under Part 3 of the Childcare Act 2006, including particulars of any previous approval or refusal of approval;

  o the name and address of any fostering service that the applicant has been an approved foster carer for in the preceding 12 months;

  o names and addresses of two persons who will provide personal references for the applicant;

  o in relation to the applicant and each member of their household aged 18 or over, an enhanced Disclosure and Barring Service (DBS) Certificate;

  o details of any current and any previous marriage, civil partnership or similar relationship.

- consult the local authority in whose area the applicant lives, if this is different from the fostering service; and

- interview at least two personal referees and prepare written reports of the interviews; or, if the person has been an approved foster carer for another fostering service in the preceding 12 months, request a written reference from that fostering service (Department of Education, 2013b, pp6–7).

Most fostering services would also interview people whom the applicant had been in an intimate relationship with in the past, following the recommendation regarding this arising from the Brighton and Hove Inquiry in 2011 into the death of John Smith, a four-year-old child placed with prospective adopters. In addition, where an applicant is or had been previously employed, a work reference. If stage one is satisfactorily completed and the information obtained leads the fostering service to surmise that the likelihood at that stage is the prospective applicant could become a capable foster carer, the fostering service moves on to stage two. Indeed the 2013 amendments to the 2011 Fostering Services Guidance and Regulations allow the possibility of stages one and two to run concurrently, if the fostering service decides that is best.

The information gathering in stage one is seen by the Department of Education to be the stage when 'basic information' is obtained, and stage two where 'more detailed information' is acquired, which has to include the following:

- details of personality;

- religious persuasion and capacity to care for a child from any particular religious persuasion;

- racial origin, cultural and linguistic background and capacity to care for a child from any particular racial origin or cultural or religious background;

- past and present employment or occupation, standard of living, leisure activity and interests;

- previous experience (if any) of caring for their own and other children;

- skills, competence and potential relevant to their capacity to care effectively for a child placed with them (Department of Education, 2013b, p8).

What needs to be considered in an assessment?

Most fostering services explore in depth more than the Department of Education requires of them, thus enabling safe enough recommendations to be made to fostering panels and the fostering service ADM, regarding whether or not someone should be approved as a foster carer, including:

- the applicant's own history and how they understand its impact upon themselves, and what the implications of that history are for their potential ability to care for foster children. This 'history' would include their individual, family and intimate relationship history;

- the applicant's experience and understanding of attachment, transition and loss, and how their experiences and understanding might shape their care of foster children;

- the applicant's potential ability to be a professional member of the team around the foster child, their ability to work with other professionals and manage the bureaucratic aspects of fostering including: keeping records, accounts of expenditure and report writing;

- the applicant's potential to work in an inclusive and facilitative manner with a foster child's family, and people significant to them;

- the applicant's ability to value and respect a foster child's own family's and community's history;

- the applicant's potential capacity to engage proactively with the education and health of a foster child, to enable that child to meet their educational potential and have their physical and mental health needs met;

- the applicant's physical and mental health and how these might impact upon their foster carer role;

- the applicant's experience of education, and their employment history;

- the applicant's financial circumstances;

- the applicant's potential to engage proactively with their community and locality, to help foster children take on sport and leisure activities, as well as help them make friends;

- the applicant's potential, as well as their own wish, to meet the needs of a range of different foster children and placement types including, for example: babies; teenagers; children with health conditions; children with physical disabilities; children with learning disabilities or parent and child placements;

- the applicant's parenting capacity. If they have parented before, and now have adult children, their children's experience of that parenting;

- if they have children living with them, those children's wishes and understanding of becoming part of a fostering family;

- if the applicant has other adults living within the home, who are not their partner or adult children, those adults' understanding of becoming part of a fostering household;

- taking into account all of the above, the applicant's potential to meet the needs of foster children, some of whom will have experienced abuse, neglect, domestic violence, drug and alcohol dependence, trafficking, war, migration, loss, and all of whom will be coping with separation;

- the applicant's potential for developing the skills, and emotional and intellectual capacity to manage difficult behaviour in a kind, boundaried, containing manner, and to use proven interventions that can change children's behaviour for the better;

- the applicant's ability to communicate with children in an age-appropriate manner, their ability to play, to be welcoming and to demonstrate warmth and encouragement;

- the applicant's practical domestic and employment circumstances: whether or not they will be able to manage the day-to-day requirements of fostering expected by the fostering service, for example taking a foster child to school or nursery each day or taking them to contact, at the same time as meeting their own, and their families', practical and emotional requirements and needs;

- an applicant's belief in the possibility of change, their degree of hopefulness and agency in the world.

The gathering of this assessment information, if the assessor has 'good enough' communication and interviewing skills, can be straightforward; the difficulty lies in making sense of the material that has been gleaned, its analysis and synthesis to enable an informed prognosis about an applicant's potential as a foster carer. Chapman rightly places emphasis on the analysis of data during assessment and argues that there should be *an emphasis on analysis of the information collected, as this is something that is often identified as lacking in assessments presented to fostering panels* (2009, p3).

Tools for undertaking assessments

Most fostering services use the BAAF Form F assessment tool (2008) as a template for undertaking foster carer assessments. Some use the Fostering Network's Skills to Foster Assessment (2010a; 2010b), which sets out a structure for undertaking and recording foster carers' assessments. One of the problems of templates is that they can be used in a reductive and formulaic fashion. Chapman's guide (2009) to undertaking a fostering assessment using the BAAF Form F sets out a range of questions that assessors should use with applicants, and questions for themselves when they analyse the data they have gathered. This text is helpful and potentially facilitates thorough assessments taking place. However, Chapman's questions could be misused. The gathering of information through the use of set questions has its limitations as it can prohibit the foster carer's narrative being told and understood in a holistic manner. Questions should be seen as prompts for the assessor to make sure that no stone has been left unturned and be asked in the context of the working relationship that has been developed, or is being developed, between the applicant and the assessor. Wilson *et al.* emphasise the importance of the relationship to enable effective assessments to be realised: *What a relationship-based approach to assessment prioritises is the creation of a meaningful professional relationship that will enhance the accuracy and effectiveness of the assessment process . . .* (2011, p285).

Luke and Sebba (2013) undertook an international literature review looking at what tools are used to assess and select foster carers, and their efficacy. As noted above the research addressing the efficacy of prospective foster carer assessment to predict later success as foster carers is thin. When looking at the usefulness of 'instruments', such as the BAAF Form F (BAAF, 2008) among many others, the authors note that there was:

> *a limitation in the validity of the instruments to 'predict the future' by linking the characteristics and competencies of new foster care applicants to later measures of success . . . In addition, many studies failed to test the predictive power of selection instruments by measuring their relationship to child safety, ability to achieve permanency, placement stability, carer retention, child well-being or other desired outcomes.*
>
> (Luke and Sebba, 2013, p5)

Pertinent to this chapter, Luke and Sebba posit the importance of using such instruments as the BAAF Form F (BAAF, 2008) or the Fostering Network's Skills to Foster Assessment (2010a; 2010b) as one component of assessment among others, and that most importantly those undertaking prospective foster carer assessments should be capable of gathering, and making sense of, information gleaned during the assessment process. They write:

> *Fostering service providers should ensure that assessors using selection instruments as part of a wider process are thoroughly trained in collecting and analysing information from a range of sources including selection instruments, observation of carer applicants in orientation/training sessions and interviews and observations undertaken in the carer home, conducted sensitively in a way that reduces bias.*

(Luke and Sebba, 2013, p6)

A BAAF text published in 1998 remains an important guide to what assessors need to consider during foster carer assessments. Although its focus is assessing for permanence, like Beesley's text (2010) it is relevant to foster carers' assessments more generally. It deals with the emotional complexity of caring for other people's children, and the attributes required in foster carers and adopters, at the assessment stage. They write that children separated from their birth families need families:

- *with attitudes that are open and flexible rather than closed and rigid;*
- *who can face sadness and loss and are not embarrassed or threatened to talk about the feelings involved;*
- *who can put the needs of children first and not feel undermined by important past relationships;*
- *who are able to look honestly at themselves and acknowledge their strengths and limitations;*
- *who do not expect to do it all on their own and can use and welcome help if it is needed.*

(BAAF Assessment Working Party, 1998, p7)

The Fostering Network's assessment guide for applicants notes the personal qualities that foster carers need. The first of these, although one would think it was obvious, is important to explicitly name:

- *enjoying the company of children and young people;*
- *good communication skills;*
- *the ability to work as part of a team;*
- *being flexible and non-judgemental;*
- *being able to negotiate and compromise;*
- *being able to understand and empathise, both with children and with their families.*

(The Fostering Network, 2010b, p9)

Schofield and Beek's work (2006) on attachment, and foster care and adoption, has been invaluable for social workers and foster carers. Their 'secure base' model and its application to the assessment of prospective foster carers is an effective model to focus the assessor and applicant's attention on the importance of particular areas related to attachment, to be explored during the assessment. I have reproduced their diagram in Figure 4.1.

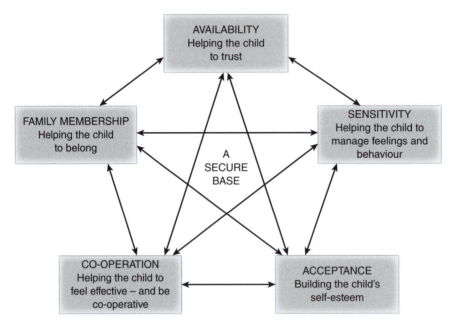

Figure 4.1   Secure base model (Schofield and Beek, UEA, 2009)

Their website is useful for social workers and foster carers, providing detailed guidance about the exploration of each area identified in their diagram above (**www.uea.ac.uk/ providingasecurebase/uses-of-the-model/the-assessment-of-prospective-foster-carers- and-adopters**).

The recommendation arising from an assessment of a prospective foster carer only ever offers a prognosis about the potential quality of care that foster carer will afford foster children, whereas a foster carer's review enables that prognosis to be tested out against the realities of the foster care provided to specific children; this is explored in Chapter 7.

Assessing sameness and difference

Foster carers are a diverse group representing most of the cultures, ethnicities and religions to be found in the UK. There are couples, single people of both genders, people with disabilities, lesbians, gay men and transgender people who are foster carers. This means that over time most social workers will work with foster carers who are different from themselves in some way. This requires what Cree and Myers (2008), among others, refer to as 'cultural competence'. In Chapter 3 we saw how the Wakefield Inquiry (Parrott *et al.*, 2007) uncovered serious misjudgements on the part of social workers, which the inquiry team associated with the social workers' desire to be seen as non-discriminatory. That desire has been linked to what is referred to as 'anti-discriminatory practice' (ADP). Fear of being discriminatory has been shown to have serious negative impacts on social workers' professional judgement. Walker and Beckett elaborate on the complexity of this when they write:

> One of the main tasks of a social worker carrying out assessments is to discriminate. Given that it is generally agreed that social work should strive to be anti-discriminatory, this sounds like an odd thing to say, but there is a difference between being discriminatory and being discriminating. Indeed, though both words refer to making distinctions, they are in some way opposites. Being discriminatory means making bad judgements on the basis of irrational prejudice. The adjective 'discriminating', however, refers to the ability to make fine judgements based on skill and knowledge.

> (Walker and Beckett, 2011, p83)

All social workers must avoid negative discrimination (as indeed they are required to by the Equality Act 2010), at the same time as utilising skills, knowledge and professional expertise to make sound judgements, which involves 'discriminating', in the sense that Walker and Beckett use the word, as well as utilising their abilities to be discerning.

The idea of 'cultural competence' also has its own pitfalls. Cree and Myers warn of the tendency to think that being taught facts about different cultures, for example, can automatically lead to cultural competence, whereas, in fact, it can result in quite the reverse, poor practice, as the unique individual is lost in a sea of cultural generalisations (2008, p46). They refer to the work of Husain (2006), who suggests that cultural competence requires social workers to have 'cultural knowledge, cultural awareness and cultural sensitivity' (2008, p46). For these to be translated into effective practice social workers need the self-awareness and emotional and intellectual capacities to process their reactions to unfamiliarity and difference, and not just to react. Featherstone and Green, writing about the usefulness of the ideas of the social and cultural theorist Judith Butler to social work practice, write:

> Butler returns us to a tradition in social work that asserts our common humanity, but, at the very same time that we recognise our humanness, she asks us to question the grounds on which we have constructed what it is to be human. She challenges us to recognise our strangeness to ourselves and our familiarity with others as well as our strangeness to others and our familiarity to ourselves.

> (Featherstone and Green, 2013, p71)

The ideas of Judith Butler are further explored in a recent edited text addressing social work's developing ideas related to what used to be referred to as anti-discriminatory practice (Cocker and Hafford-Letchfield, forthcoming).

'Culture' has many denotations, and those meanings have changed over time. When discussed in social work circles it is often a word used in such a manner that connects it subliminally to a 'thing' or 'things' black and ethnic minority communities 'have', rather than being something related and relevant to all people. The word's use has changed from its original Latin derivation's meaning, to its use in nineteenth-century anthropology, when it evolved to refer to the distinct ways that people lived differently from one another, and the symbolic meaning of their various practices. Indeed the association of 'culture' being something that black and ethnic minority peoples 'have', rather than it being relevant to all peoples, irrespective of nation or ethnic origin, has been argued to be a potentially racist hangover from when anthropological interest in this area was predominantly white anthropologists studying people that they defined as 'other'.

Another use of the term 'culture', where it is used to refer to 'cultivation' and 'improvement', has been used to describe what can be loosely termed as the 'arts' and people's interest in them. A person in 1950 might have been described as 'cultured', and their contemporaries would have understood that to mean that they were knowledgeable about, and familiar with, certain art forms; for example, painting, literature, sculpture, ballet, opera, theatre, etc. Where the term was, and is still, used in this context, it was/is usually associated with an assumption that the middle and upper classes owned/own 'culture' and the working class lacks it. This ownership of 'culture', by the middle and upper classes, has been challenged globally in many forms. We now understand art forms to encompass much more than those listed above including 'street culture', graffiti and many varied expressions of creativity and imagination. Many of these art forms were developed, like black jazz, gospel music and Tyree Guyton's Detroit Heidelberg 'Art' Project (Guyton, 2013), as forms of resistance.

In both the uses of the term 'culture' I have described, the first, where it is used to denote practices associated with certain ethnicities, and the second, where it refers to creative activities, and the appreciation of artistic forms, the term has been historically related to power relations. So when we talk about 'cultural competence' this involves a complex, political and nuanced set of activities with which we expect social workers to engage. Cultural competence is not about knowing distilled information about the social and cultural practices of a particular ethnic group, which can lead to negative and positive stereotyped shorthand understandings developing in social work practice. Rule writes that *a recurrent message from all studies is the need to avoid stereotypical views and unwarranted assumptions regarding prospective minority ethnic carers and their varying family patterns* (2006, p15).

A simple way to start, for those undertaking assessments of prospective foster carers, is to understand, first, that all people, families and communities 'have' and 'do' culture, even when they are not necessarily able to define or articulate what it is or involves. White families living in Grindleford in Derbyshire have, and do, culture, as do Punjabi Sikh families living in Wolverhampton. All people/families have rituals that historically, and currently, have helped, and help them manage the powerful emotions connected to survival and existence; rituals associated with: food; desire; sex; relationships; forming stable family and kinship groups; the birth of children; transitions related to human development, for example the transition from childhood to adulthood; loss; and death. Second, we need an awareness of, and understanding about, how our own 'culture' informs our view of the world, individuals and families, and how the implications of this 'informing' influences our assessment practice when considering the suitability of an individual or family to care for foster children.

Understanding the 'culture' of a prospective fostering household is essential for an informed judgement to be made about a foster child's potential to thrive in that home. Assessors require the confidence, humility and purposeful interviewing skills to facilitate the prospective foster carer to tell their story about their own, their family's and their community's sense of their ethnicity, culture and religion, where this is relevant. Most importantly the assessor has to elicit from them their unique relationship to their 'culture', and what that means for their sense of self, family and community, and how all of that impacts upon their potential care of foster children. This is an essential part of assessment of foster carers irrespective of their ethnicity, religion or national origin. In addition, as noted above, as social work practitioners we have to acquire an awareness and understanding of the temporal and spatial specificity of our own experience and 'culture' to have an appreciation of each individual and family being different, even when they seem to be similar in a number of regards. By the assessor enacting interest in, and respect for, the foster carer and the complexity of their story, when undertaking this work with prospective foster carers, we model how they could, in future, respect and value the unique histories and family cultures of foster children joining them.

An area of social work that has received less attention than when social workers engage with individuals and families who are perceived as 'different' from themselves in some way, whether it be sexual orientation, age, gender, nationality, language, religion or ethnicity, is when social workers work with individuals and families that are superficially thought to be similar to, or the same as, the social worker, for example when a Bangladeshi social worker assesses a Bangladeshi couple who hope to foster, or when a white English social worker assesses a white, single English man. There is a danger that when the social worker lacks an in-depth understanding of the specificity of their own history, family, community and related relationships they can inadvertently presuppose that the person, or people, they are assessing share their experience, perceptions and feelings. Of course, in some instances, there are shared experiences, for example, the Bangladeshi social worker and the couple being assessed are likely to share the experience of migration to the UK, either personally or in relatively recent generations. However, each person's experience of that migratory journey and process, although sharing some aspects of that experience with others, will be unique. It is the experience itself, in relation to the person's own personality, life experience and family group, that will have lasting meaning for how migration has built upon the individual's history, experience, strengths and vulnerabilities.

It is important for us to remember that in a time that makes much of appreciating 'diversity and difference', partly as a social and political response to managing the complex political, social and emotional aftermath of the history of colonial and imperial relationships, direct oppression and prejudice, human beings have much in common, irrespective of their nationality, ethnicity, religion, age, ability/disability, gender or sexuality. It is an awareness of our commonality, as much as our differences, that helps capable foster carers have the emotional and intellectual capacity to make meaningful connections with foster children. Love, attachment, desire, commitment, pride, anger, loss, sadness and disappointment are all human emotions that are shared by everyone, irrespective of our social, geographical or temporal location. Effective social work practice in assessing applicants involves the capacity to see beyond the cultural norms and practices that we all enact, at the same time as respecting and valuing them, where they are benevolent, and get to the core of what is being felt, lived and experienced. To get 'to the core' social work assessors and foster carers alike require passionate curiosity about people and their stories; without it as a prerequisite they are unlikely to be effective.

CASE STUDY 4.1

Tom works in a local authority team in the south-west of England. He has been qualified as a social worker for four years but his assessment of Jim and Samantha Thomas, as prospective foster carers, is the first he has undertaken. The assessment seemed to be going well, from his and their perspectives. However, Tom had been aware of not being able to get Jim, and particularly Samantha, to think very deeply about how they would care for foster children who were of a different nationality, ethnicity or religion from themselves. They described themselves at the start of the assessment as a white, British, middle-aged, Church of England, working-class, heterosexual couple, who had no children. Tom also knew there was a gap in his knowledge about Samantha's maternal grandparents, now both dead, who she said she knew little about, and had no contact with when she was a child.

During the assessment Jim and Samantha attended the Skills to Foster preparatory training programme. In their report the Skills to Foster trainers fed back to Tom that they thought Samantha was slightly dismissive about the importance of children having a positive sense of their heritage. This increased Tom's unease, and he realised he needed to address this area more explicitly with Tom and Samantha. His initial reaction, when he read the trainers' report, was to feel hostile, for the first time, towards Samantha who up until now he had experienced as warm and open. If she felt like that about the lack of importance for children about their heritage, when that was different from her own, what were her real thoughts about him as a black man of African-Caribbean descent? Tom talked with his supervisor about his thoughts and feelings. They agreed that on his next visit he would focus on this area of their assessment, and that he should engage with them, as he had done until now, warmly, empathetically and purposefully explaining why this was an important area to discuss with them as prospective foster carers.

Because of Tom's ability to engage helpfully with Jim and Samantha, he was able to have a full and open discussion with them. Samantha started the session by being quite angry about the comments from the Skills to Foster trainers, and she said that they had misunderstood her. She also tried to justify her position by emphasising her belief that integration of black and ethnic minority communities into British 'culture' was important, and focusing on difference was unhelpful. As the discussion progressed Tom sensed a new disquiet in Samantha, conveyed by her body language and facial expression; at one point Tom thought she was going to cry. Tom knew it was important to talk directly with Samantha regarding what he observed, rather than pretending he had not noticed her upset expression. When he did she bent forward crying. Jim seemed confused by Samantha's behaviour, but went over to where she was sitting to comfort her.

Tom realised that Jim did not seem to know why Samantha was so upset. After she recovered herself she began to talk. It transpired that Samantha's mum had never discussed her family when Samantha was growing up, and if she asked anything about them she was always 'fobbed off' by her mum. The story was that Samantha's mum had left home at 15 years of age to work on a farm in Devon, and had no contact with her family since. She said that this was because they had not got on. However, when Samantha was 14, during a row with her dad, he had shouted at Samantha saying she was 'just like your mum's family, devious and not to be trusted'. When Samantha approached her mum after this row, her mum was upset and did eventually talk to Samantha.

It transpired that Samantha's mum was of English gypsy descent, something that she had hidden from Samantha's dad when they met when she was 18 years of age. He was hostile towards gypsies and travellers, holding prejudiced and stereotypical views, and Samantha's mum's heritage became a hidden taboo subject. It transpired that Samantha's mum had lost both her parents to cancer in her early teens and she, as their only child, had been taken in by her uncle's large family on the site that her extended family occupied in Worcestershire. She had left at 15 because she felt excluded by her uncle's children, who she had never got on well with. Over the years she kept in contact with her aunt by telephone until she died in 2000.

This information was as new to Jim as it was to Tom. Because of this they agreed with Tom's manager they would put their prospective foster carer assessment on hold for three months while Jim and Samantha had time to integrate this new knowledge into their relationship. Samantha also needed time to consider the impact on her, and her future role as a foster carer, of having internalised a negative view of her heritage, such that it had remained hidden from even those closest to her.

In those three months Tom visited Jim and Samantha to assess how they were progressing, and encouraged Samantha to make contact with a gypsy and traveller organisation in the city near to where they lived. Tom emphasised the potential strength of Samantha's heritage, and the process she had recently experienced of having to make explicit previously hidden material from her and her family's past, particularly in helping foster children who might themselves have negative feelings associated with their heritage. However, Tom knew he would need to weigh up when he resumed their assessment how Samantha was integrating this new shared knowledge into her day-to-day lived experience, regarding herself, and her relationship with Jim, and others, to consider how this might enhance or detract from her potential as a foster carer.

Recruiting and assessing particular groups of foster carers

Ethnicity, nationality and religion

From reading the above section it could be assumed that I am arguing that at the end of the day all human beings are the same, and therefore any foster child can be placed with any foster family, and all will be well. It follows from that position that prospective foster carers can all be recruited and assessed in exactly the same way. This is not what I am saying. What we share as human beings is fundamentally important, but because of the history of colonial and imperial relationships, direct oppression and prejudice, there are some matters that have to be considered when we are recruiting and assessing foster carers.

In 2012 the UK journal, *Adoption and Fostering*, dedicated an issue to multiculturalism, identity and family placement, and although the majority of papers were related to adoption, much of the content was of interest to foster carers and social workers working in the field of foster care (BAAF, 2012). The England Guidance for foster carer assessment dictates that assessors have to 'obtain information' from prospective foster carers about their *racial origin, cultural and linguistic background and capacity to care for a child from any particular racial origin or cultural or religious background* (Department of Education, 2013b, p8). This requirement was formulated against the backdrop of a history in social work in the UK, since the 1980s, of the arguments for and against what was referred to as 'same race placements', i.e. the idea that children of a particular ethnicity should be placed with a family of the same ethnicity. Much of this thinking was informed by the experiences of black and ethnic minority children who had grown up in white families, and the belief that to develop a strong sense of self, and positive identity, a child should be placed in a family of the same ethnicity and/or religion. These ideas were contested, but 'same race placements' ideology and practice dominated fostering and adoption for many years. In its worst manifestations the ethnicity of a child in public care was sometimes the only consideration when thinking about matching them with a fostering or adoptive family.

The social work and foster care context in which 'same race placements' flourished was one where the vast majority of white children were placed with white foster families, who were themselves the majority of the foster carer population in all areas of the UK. When 'race' and ethnicity were discussed it was only in connection to black and ethnic minority children needing placements, who at that time (the 1980s) were predominately of African-Caribbean or mixed heritage, African-Caribbean and white UK descent. The context today is very different, although those same children remain over-represented in public care (Barn and Kirton, 2012). The ethnic, religious and national make-up of the children looked after population has changed significantly in the last 30 years.

Today the idea of a 'same race placement' for a child of Portuguese, Roma and Pakistani heritage poses challenges. Rather, in foster care the move has been away from 'same race placements', towards an urgent requirement to recruit a range of foster carers from every ethnic, religious and national community in the UK, who will have the emotional and intellectual capacity to keep alive, both psychologically and practically, the family, ethnic, national and religious, where it is relevant, heritage of a foster child. This applies to a white foster carer, caring for a foster child who is defined as 'black or ethnic minority', or a foster carer who defines themselves as black British, African-Caribbean caring for a 'white' foster child. This is not to underplay the importance of black and ethnic minority children, in my view, wherever possible, without causing placement delay, or over-prioritising ethnicity/religion/nationality over and above a holistic assessment of all their needs, being placed within a family that feels as familiar to them as possible. This familiarity is also important for white children, but in their case the wider society reflects back to them, in part, much that is familiar.

The current reality is that some foster children's accurate ethnic/national/religious heritage is unknown, or so complex that a 'match' would be unlikely. We therefore need to make sure that all prospective foster carer assessments consider the applicant's understanding of caring for a child of a different heritage from their own, and what valuing, respecting and keeping alive a foster child's ethnic/national/religious heritage actually means, in terms of the day-to-day care of that foster child. In addition, how the applicant imagines they will work in an inclusive way with a foster child's family, while keeping their foster child safe and central to all considerations, has to be explored.

I have referred in this to prospective foster carers' 'emotional and intellectual' capacity to meet foster children's varied needs. I use 'intellectual' deliberately, as prospective foster carers need the cognitive, as well as emotional, ability to understand concepts like 'deprivation', 'marginalisation' and 'racism', and how they impact on foster children and their families. I am not arguing that prospective foster carers have to understand these concepts at the point of applying to be foster carers, but rather that they have the potential and openness to grasp ideas over time with supervision, and a personal development plan. Most important is their potential ability to apply an understanding of concepts such as 'racism' to lived practice in foster care.

CASE STUDY 4.2

What will a foster carer need to do and say to equip a 16-year-old young man with Mozambique and white South African heritage who is fostered, to manage the aftermath of a racist incident?

Joel was waiting for a London Underground train at 10 p.m. one night on his way home. He had just come from a sixth form concert where he had successfully played his cello in public, for the first time, and was feeling excited and proud. His Eritrean foster carer had not been able to be at the concert, because that evening she had to accompany another of her foster children to hospital, because she had taken an overdose of painkillers. His dad and half-brother had been at the concert, and they had got on well that evening, which had not been the case every time they met. While waiting five minutes for his train to Barking he was taunted by a group of drunk, young white women. He tried to ignore them and moved away from where they were standing to the other end of the platform. One man, on the platform, told them to stop. Although Joel was pleased, on one level, about the man's helpful intervention, he found the other passengers looking at what was going on excruciating. When he got home his response was to be angry and hostile to his foster carer, and swear at and kick the family cat, of which he was very fond. He said that he thought playing the cello was pointless, and that he would not use public transport again.

How might his foster carer work with Joel to help him manage this experience of racism? This scenario and related question is as relevant for a prospective foster carer assessor to

(Continued)

use when assessing black and ethnic minority prospective foster carers as it is with white foster carers. Many black and ethnic minority foster carers will have managed racism in their own lives, but might not have helped a young person manage his own reactions. Prospective white UK foster carers have to have the imagination, and emotional capacity, to feel what it would be like to be at the receiving end of racism, and then think how they might helpfully respond to Joel.

Lesbian and gay prospective foster carers

Foster care is an area of social work practice that provokes strong feelings about families, children, relationships and attachment. We all have our own ideas regarding what is best for children, and particularly for foster children who have already been removed from their birth families. Because of this, social workers need a sound knowledge base about what children actually need to enable their physical, emotional and educational development, and for them to reach their individual potentials. This knowledge enables assessors to work from a professional position rather than relying on their own personal opinions and prejudices. Social work assessors are today in a better informed moment regarding research informing us about how children fare in lesbian and gay households (Golombok, 2000; Patterson, 2005; Hicks, 2011; Mellish, Jennings, Tasker, Lamb and Golombok, 2013).

The recruitment, assessment and approval of lesbian and gay foster carers are areas of social work practice that historically have been contested. The political and social context for lesbians and gay men in the UK has changed considerably since the 1970s, in part in response to lesbians' and gay men's growth in confidence, and as a result influence on social policy. Together the Adoption and Children Act 2002 and the Equality Act 2010 require lesbian and gay fostering and adoption applicants to be treated equitably by adoption and fostering agencies (Brown, 2008; Brown and Cocker, 2008; Brown and Kershaw, 2008). However, this is not as straightforward as it seems. Some argue that lesbians and gay men should be assessed in exactly the same way as their heterosexual counterparts. Others argue that because of lesbians' and gay men's historical marginalisation and oppression, how this has impinged on them and their relationships with others should be considered during the assessment process, because this potentially has implications for how they will care for foster children (Brown, 1991; Mallon and Betts, 2005; Brown and Cocker, 2008; Cocker and Brown, 2010).

Since 1991 I have been developing a model for assessing lesbians and gay men, and since 2008 have continued this development with Christine Cocker from the University of East Anglia. In 2011 we published the SPRIINT model to facilitate discussion with applicants of matters that we think important when assessing lesbian and gay foster carers and adopters. We argue that in addition to what we refer to as the 'generic assessment', i.e. the material covered in this chapter up to this point, we should, with lesbian and gay applicants, in addition consider particular areas.

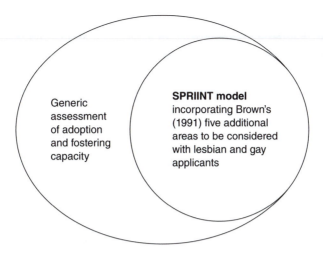

Figure 4.2   SPRIINT model (Cocker and Brown, 2010, p27)

In the process of developing this model, specific to the assessment of lesbians and gay men, it became apparent to us that it was also applicable to prospective foster carer and adopter assessments more generally, because sexuality and intimate relationships are important areas of applicants' lives, enacted in the domestic sphere, impacting on foster children, and need exploring in all assessments. However, the SPRIINT model started life for use when assessing lesbian and gay prospective foster carers and adopters. We have argued that every aspect of SPRIINT should be explored when assessing lesbian and gay applicants to enable a full holistic assessment to be undertaken, and an informed recommendation to be made to the fostering panel as to whether or not they should be approved as foster carers.

SPRIINT is an acronym which stands for:

- Sexual orientation

- Previous sexual relationship histories

- Relationships (current)

- Intimacy (the expression of this with each other)

- Integration into the community

- Not so nice bits (digging below the surface; exploring the long-term nature of relationships; coping with difficulties, stress, disagreements, etc.)

- Think: about the patterns and the gaps within the stories being told.

(Cocker and Brown, 2010, p26)

One of the strengths that capable lesbian and gay foster carers can bring to fostering, which they share with other groups that have been oppressed and marginalised, is their potential ability to understand foster children's feelings of marginalisation. As Mallon and Betts note, many lesbians and gay men have experienced discrimination and can empathise with children who are looked after feeling marginalised (Mallon and Betts, 2005).

Earlier in this chapter I wrote about the dangers of an 'ADP' approach to social work practice when it lacks discernment, discrimination and professional judgement. Some social workers have been anxious about assessing lesbians and gay men for fear of being accused of being homophobic; similarly some have been anxious assessing applicants of a different ethnicity or religion from themselves for fear of being accused of being racist or discriminatory. However, when a social worker has undertaken a well-evidenced assessment, when they have engaged effectively with the applicants, in which every aspect of an applicant's life, relationships and household has been scrutinised, and their potential to care for foster children explored, where judgements have been informed by research findings, those social workers should be confident about their professional judgement and their recommendation to the fostering panel about whether or not someone ought to be approved as a foster carer.

Chapter summary

- Assessment is the start, for most applicants, of their relationship with a fostering service and their fostering career.

- A foster carer's experience of the assessment should be one that models warmth, openness, trust, clarity, purposeful interviewing and an effective professional relationship. This should be one in which there has been an exploration of the foster carer's story, and the implications of that story for them as potential foster carers, where the detail of their day-to-day life, as well as their potential capacity to care for foster children, has been rigorously investigated and evaluated in relation to their potential to become capable foster carers.

- A relationship of warmth, trust, integrity and openness should be the hallmark of the applicant/assessor relationship. This is a complex matter because we ask applicants to be open and honest with their assessor but sometimes when they are open and honest, and as a result disclose problematic information, we make a professional judgement that they are not suitable to be foster carers.

- The nature of the assessor and applicant relationship, because the assessment takes place in the applicant's home, because the content of the material is intimate and powerful, means that there is potential for the assessor/applicant relationship to become enmeshed. Hence, the importance of supervision for assessors, to make sure that the assessor has the opportunity to reflect on their assessment practice, and is enabled to analyse and synthesise the material they elicit.

- It is relatively common for foster carer assessors to form a view early on as to the suitability of the applicant to become a foster carer. The danger then is that the assessor seeks out and only hears material that fits their positive view of the applicant, and as a result plays down information that contradicts their positive and over-optimistic perspective. This is not a criticism of assessors, but rather acknowledges a potential inevitable dynamic that needs to be addressed in supervision. This can be facilitated in part by the supervisor asking the assessor to look for evidence that counters their own position, so that a balanced and properly informed professional judgement can eventually be reached.

- Areas of social work practice covered in this chapter are re-visited in later chapters, in the same way as material elicited during a foster carer's assessment should be re-visited throughout their fostering career, in their annual reviews and in ongoing work they do with their SSW in supervision, explored in the following chapter.

FURTHER READING

Schofield, G and Beek, M (2009) *Providing a Secure Base.* Norwich: The University of East Anglia, www.uea.ac.uk/providingasecurebase/uses-of-the-model/the-assessment-of-prospective-foster-carers-and-adopters

Beesley P (2010) *Making Good Assessments: A Practical Resource Guide.* London: BAAF.

The above two publications provide both theoretical and practice guidance about assessing prospective foster carers.

The Fostering Network (2010b) *The Skills to Foster Assessment. Assessing Foster Carers: A Social Worker's Guide.* London: The Fostering Network.

This publication complements the Fostering Network's model for assessing foster carers and in doing so provides the reader with useful material to consider.

Luke, N and Sebba, J (2013) *How Are Foster Carers Selected? An International Literature Review of Instruments Used within Foster Carer Selection.* Oxford: Rees Centre, University of Oxford.

The above international literature review examines what instruments there are available to facilitate the assessment of prospective foster carers, as well as considering the evidence regarding their efficacy.

Chapter 5

Supervision and support of foster carers

CHAPTER OBJECTIVES

By the end of this chapter, readers should:

- be familiar with what is involved in the social work supervision and support of foster carers;
- understand what research findings tell us about this area of social work practice;
- appreciate how our own social work practice with foster carers can be built on to make sure that foster carers are supervised and supported in such a way that enables them to offer foster children positive, reparatory family care.

Introduction

Nutt, drawing on others' research findings and her own interviews with 46 foster carers, appositely titled her book *The Lives of Foster Carers: Private Sacrifices, Public Restrictions* (2006). Becoming a foster carer involves the carer's previously private domestic sphere becoming public space, impacting not just on the foster carer or the fostering couple, but on their children and others who might live in their home. Stating the obvious, foster care takes place in the intimate family space of private homes, and supervision of foster carers takes place in this private/public space.

As noted earlier, in recent years at any one time approximately 75 per cent of children who are looked after by the State are placed with foster carers, which means that, as an understatement, the quality of the foster care is important for the overall good of children placed in public care. At its best foster care offers the opportunity for children to have a reparatory family experience, providing a safe space in which to develop their potential, continue their relationships with people significant to them, develop new ones with their foster carer and their family and friends, enhance their sense of their own and their family's histories, improve their health, engage productively with education and, for some, to be enabled to manage their difficulties, and sometimes problematic behaviour, with the foster carer's and other professionals' help.

Given the number of foster children and fostering households in the UK, the quality control of placements provided by local authorities, charities and independent and private organisations is a complex matter. The Guidance and Regulations (HM Government, 2011; Department of Education, 2011b; Department of Education, 2013b) and the NMS (Department of Education, 2011a) provide a benchmark for what is expected of foster carers and their fostering services. However, how these requirements are applied varies, as evidenced by the differing outcomes of OFSTED inspection reports of fostering services. The SSW plays a central role in the quality assurance of fostering, as well as co-ordinating support needed by foster carers to help them care for children (Lawson, 2011a).

Nutt's interviewees articulated the most important message for all those involved in foster care, that foster children are the focus and priority. Discussing her foster carer interviewees she writes, *the striking feature is that although the carers are a diverse, heterogeneous group, their views, experiences and constructions are consistent across interviews – foster children are their priority* (2006, p2). The foster child is central and must be the focus of all those working with them, most particularly the foster carer and their SSW.

Given the role of the SSW is pivotal in ensuring the quality of foster care generally, and specifically for each child in respect of ensuring that the fostering aspects of a child's care plan are met, it is surprising that it has attracted minimal academic or research attention. Indeed there is little written about what SSWs actually do when they work with foster carers. An exception to this observation is Lawson's book (2011b) written for SSWs, examining the detail of the SSW's role and making links with the Guidance and Regulations (HM Government, 2010; HM Government, 2011) and the NMS (Department of Education, 2011a).

Interestingly, from the research that has been done, usually undertaken as part of a wider study looking at more than the role of the SSW, there are mixed messages regarding if the amount and quality of supervision and support afforded foster carers makes a difference to outcomes for foster children. Research findings differ as to whether or not it makes a difference (Sinclair, 2005). There are studies that show it does make a difference, particularly in relation to the care of teenagers (Farmer, Moyers and Lipscombe, 2004). In addition, in her recent literature review looking at permanence Boddy writes, *the research reviewed here shows that support for carers, and for birthparents, and attention to children's wishes are critical to ensure quality and continuity in placements* (2013, p30). Support to foster carers and contact with their SSWs have been shown to make a difference to their retention (Wilson, Sinclair, Taylor, Pithouse and Sellick, 2004).

Although some of the research findings differ, regarding whether or not social work support to, and supervision of, foster carers impacts on outcomes for fostered children and young people, there is consensus that the term 'support', despite its ubiquitous use, is rarely defined (Harlow and Blackburn, 2011). Sinclair identified the following as 'support's' core components: finance; training and preparation; carer groups; social work support; night duty teams; short breaks; preparation for placements; and teamwork (Sinclair, 2005, pp107–11). The focus of this chapter is social work support, or rather what I refer to as supervision, which incorporates some components of support identified by Sinclair.

This chapter covers

- What the Standards, Guidance and Regulations say
- The SSW/foster carer supervisory relationship
- Supervision
- Support and development
- Child-focused reparatory care
- Placement planning
- Team around the child
- Contact
- Foster children moving on
- Managing allegations
- Valuing and developing a child's heritage/positive sense of self
- Permanence.

What the Standards, Guidance and Regulations say

The Guidance and Regulations (HM Government, 2011) briefly set out the expectations for the role of the SSW: *It is the SSW's role to supervise the foster carer's work, to ensure that they are meeting the child's needs, and to offer support and a framework to assess the foster carer's performance and develop their skills* (HM Government, 2011, p51). This is reiterated in Standard 21 of the NMS (Department of Education, 2011a, pp42–3). The formal supervisory nature of the SSW and foster carer relationship is noted in the NMS 21.8:

> *Meetings have a clear purpose and provide the opportunity to supervise the foster carer's work, ensure the foster carer is meeting the child's needs, taking into account the child's wishes and feelings, and offer support and a framework to assess the carer's performance and develop their competencies and skills.*

> (Department of Education, 2011a, p43)

The SSW/foster carer supervisory relationship
Supervision

In 2012 there were at least three books published in the UK about the role of supervision in social work (Howe and Gray, 2012; Mckitterick, 2012; Wonnacot, 2012). The Social Work Reform Board's review of social work and social work education, undertaken from 2010, necessitated a renewed focus on the importance of supervision in social work. Morrison and Wonnacott's paper on supervision summarises the key components of supervision contributing to its effectiveness. The paper is about supervision of social workers and whether it contributes to outcomes for service users; however, it can also be applied to SSWs' supervision of fosters carers and the influence this might have on outcomes for foster children. They write:

> *The limited research that exists into the impact of supervision on outcomes for service users indicates that supervision also needs to be grounded within a secure professional relationship where the supervisor takes time to understand and assess the supervisee's strengths and weaknesses. Professional practice and worker/service user dynamics need to be critically analysed, and the impact of the worker's emotions on thoughts and actions explored. This is the basis by which reflective but authoritative social work/care practice is developed.*

> (Morrison and Wonnacott, 2010)

The Foster Carers' Charter makes clear the dual responsibility of fostering services to, first, maintain the focus on the foster child, at the same time as supporting foster carers. Both these responsibilities, placed on fostering services, have to be enacted by their SSWs when they work with foster carers delivering both supervision and support. 'Children come first' is rightly the first heading of the Foster Carers' Charter (Department of Education, 2011c). The Charter emphasises the purpose of foster care as being to meet the emotional, cognitive, educational, social and physical needs and aspirations of foster children.

> *Children in foster care deserve to experience as full a family life as possible as part of a loving foster family with carers who can make everyday decisions as they would with their own child and without the child feeling that they 'stand out' as a looked after child.*

> *Children must be given every support to develop their own identities and aspirations, fulfil their potential and take advantage of all opportunities to promote their talents and skills. Above all, they should be listened to.*

> (Department of Education, 2011c, p2)

To help foster carers enable children, in their care, to experience warm, containing and facilitative family life requires a fostering service to also 'take care' of its foster carers. The same document states the Department of Education's intention in this regard; that fostering services:

> *Treat foster carers with openness, fairness and respect as a core member of the team around the child and support them in making reasonable and appropriate decisions on behalf of their foster child.*

> (Department of Education, 2011c, p2)

The relationship between a foster carer and their SSW is therefore a complex one, but is primarily supervisory in nature. The complexity lies for the SSW in balancing the often close nature of the working relationship, with its inbuilt requirement to offer support, with retaining a critical eye, and a probing supervisory approach, making sure that foster carers are both enabled to, and actually do, care well for their foster children. There can be a tension for both the SSW and the foster carer between the supervision and support roles, which sometimes comes to the fore when an allegation is made against a foster carer, or a standard of care matter raised by a third party. The SSW's primary focus is the foster child. Their role is crucial in facilitating the enhancement of the quality of foster care and thus the quality of life for foster children.

Lawson lists the key components of supervision of foster carers, to enable such a child focus as:

> *providing information, advice and guidance; reviewing practical and emotional support needs; checking standards of care; responding to comments, concerns and allegations; ensuring compliance with policies and procedures; noting significant events and changes to the household; managing risk, health and safety and ensuring safer care; reviewing implementation of care plans for each child in placement; monitoring impact of fostering on the household; responding to carers' feedback and concerns; identifying and supporting learning and development needs; reviewing current and future use of resources; checking payments and equipment; reviewing records and reviewing carer's relationship with children placed.*

> (Lawson, 2011b, p37)

Supervision sessions should be regular and recorded, and the foster carer given a copy as well as them being stored on the fostering service's filing system. I argue below that Lawson's last component *reviewing carer's relationship with children placed* should be a central focus of supervision, and one that is proactively and regularly addressed to enable foster children to develop their potential and emotional well-being.

CASE STUDY 5.1

Sarah is a full-time, single foster carer who settled in England from Zimbabwe in 2003. She has two children, Tammy who is nine, and Jason who is seven years of age. Since she was approved as a foster carer, four years ago, she has fostered four babies who she successfully helped move on to adoptive families. She is currently caring for Timmy, an 18-month-old, mixed-heritage, Jamaican, Scottish toddler, who is subject to care proceedings and is currently placed with her on an Interim Care Order. Sarah, knowing some of Timmy's mum's history, assumed that Timmy would be placed for adoption, as it seemed unlikely to her that he would be returned to his mum's care. However, in the last month Timmy's mum's brother, Timmy's uncle Errol, and his partner Jen, have come forward as potential special guardians for Timmy.

Sarah, on getting this information from Timmy's social worker, felt sceptical about their ability to care for Timmy, and thought they had only put themselves forward because they believed they would get some sort of financial allowance, as part of a Special

Guardianship Order Support Plan. Sarah thought Timmy, who she had fostered for more than four months and was fond of, would be better off with adopters.

Sarah has an open and straightforward supervisory relationship with her SSW Jane, and is someone who says exactly what she thinks, in sometimes less than diplomatic ways. One of the benefits of Sarah's seemingly blunt manner is that Jane can work with her in an open manner; nothing is ever hidden. Jane realises that she knows less about Special Guardianship Orders than she does about Adoption Orders, so makes sure she familiarises herself with best practice guidance (Simmonds, 2011) so she can help Sarah with the differences between Special Guardianship Orders and Adoption Orders, as well as the similarities. Ultimately both Orders are about permanence for Timmy.

The outcome of the special guardianship assessment for Errol and Jen is successful; the local authority is supporting their Special Guardianship Order application. Jane and Sarah attend a planning meeting with Timmy's social worker to consider the introduction of Errol and Jen to Timmy, to take place in Sarah's home over a ten-day period. Timmy has not seen Errol or Jen since he was four months old.

During the introduction Sarah keeps careful records of what happens each day, which she e-mails to Jane and Timmy's social worker, as agreed. Both Jane and Timmy's social worker detect a slightly over-critical tone in the recordings, and realise that they need to explore with Sarah whether she is picking up on real concerns about Errol and Jen, or if something else is going on. They agree that Jane will visit Sarah that evening to discuss this with her, before Errol and Jen visit for their fourth day the following morning.

When Jane visits Sarah it becomes apparent that Sarah has retained her negative view about special guardianship compared to adoption. She is also concerned about whether or not this couple, who are in their mid-twenties, will be able to cope with Timmy's long-term care. 'What will their attitude to him be if they have their own children?' From the discussion Jane is left unsure as to whether Sarah is just negative about the possibility of Timmy being subject to a Special Guardianship Order rather than an Adoption Order, or if she is detecting real concerns. She agrees with Timmy's social worker, Sarah, Errol and Jen that she will visit Sarah while Errol and Jen are at Sarah's house the following day.

Jane, on her arrival at Sarah's house, is immediately struck by Errol and Jen's maturity and warmth towards Timmy. Timmy is responsive to them, and they are engaging well with him. They have already, with Sarah's help, taken over much of his direct care in Sarah's house, as would be expected during the introductory period. They seem to relate effectively to Sarah, and are keeping to all the agreed expectations set for them by Timmy's social worker for this introductory phase.

In a telephone conversation with Sarah later that day Jane relays her view that Errol and Jen seem to be doing well, establishing a solid relationship with their nephew Timmy. Jane is clear with Sarah that she needs to make sure that her recordings reflect what she

(Continued)

Belfast Metropolitan College
Millfield LRC

CASE STUDY **5.1** *continued*

observes, and what happens each day, rather than her personal opinions. Sarah concedes that Jane is right.

By the time Timmy goes to live with Errol and Jen, Sarah and her children, although sad, because they will miss him, are happy for Timmy, Errol and Jen. Errol and Jen relay to Timmy's social worker that they found Sarah really helpful, and have since kept in touch with her because they are aware that she has been an important person in Timmy's short life to date.

Comment

- As the SSW Jane had to balance her 'support' to Sarah at the same time as being able to challenge her perception of a situation. Direct observation in this case helped Jane to get a better sense of Errol and Jen's developing relationship with Timmy.

- The introduction work foster carers do with children they foster when they move on to permanent carers is important, whether those carers be adopters, special guardians, family members or permanent foster carers. Careful, well-planned, supported and caring introductions can help children make as smooth a transition as possible from a foster placement to their permanent carers.

- Most foster carers and SSWs are more familiar currently with Adoption Orders than they are with Special Guardianship Orders; this means that the onus lies with the SSW to inform themselves about what is known about special guardianship (Simmonds, 2011) so that they can use this material in their supervision with their foster carers, when this is relevant.

- Foster carer recording is an important aspect of their role and can be usefully drawn upon in their supervision, making sure that it is accurate and apposite for its purpose.

- Helping children move on is a hard, complex piece of work and foster carers should get direct support from both the child's social worker and their SSW during the introductory period, and after their foster child moves on to their permanent family.

Support and development: child-focused reparatory care

To effectively develop the skills and knowledge of foster carers, SSWs in turn have to work in fostering services that value their professional and practice development; indeed the Guidance and Regulations requires them to do so (HM Government, 2011). To deliver supervision grounded in what is known about the variables that influence effective foster care, the SSW should have a commitment to being research informed, and have access to and be familiar with the knowledge we have about foster care. SSWs are in a much happier position, in this regard, than their predecessors, because there are now a number of research finding reviews published from 1997 that, taken together, give a solid grounding in what is currently known about foster care, and outcomes for foster children (Berridge, 1997; Schofield, 2003; Sellick, Thoburn and Philpot, 2004; Wilson *et al.*, 2004; Sinclair, 2005; Sellick, 2006; Boddy, 2013).

The SSW has to help develop a foster carers' fostering capability and skills (HM Government, 2011, p43). It is the responsibility of the SSW to produce a personal development plan (PDP) with each of their foster carers, reviewed annually at the foster carer's review (Department of Education, 2012b). For the PDP to be useful, and not just a paper exercise, the development of the PDP needs to be a collaborative exercise. The PDP will identify training that the SSW and foster carer think will facilitate the development of the foster carer's skills and knowledge, and in turn enhance the quality of their foster care, and as a result the foster child's experience. However, training is only one aspect of development. Much development activity is delivered by the SSW through supervision, as it is here that the day-to-day ongoing foster care practice with specific children can be worked with, and hopefully enhanced.

To maintain and build upon the beneficial effect on foster care of such training programmes as KEEP, or Fostering Changes (Chapter 6), particularly regarding managing children's problematic emotions and behaviour, the key messages and learning from such programmes need to be re-visited by the SSW in supervision. For example, this would be relevant for an SSW supervising a foster carer who is managing the chaotic behaviour of a 12-year-old girl who has been sexually exploited, or helping three siblings aged four, seven and nine be less aggressive to one another, or encouraging a 14-year-old young man to lessen his cannabis and alcohol consumption, or stop a traumatised six year old, who has witnessed too much domestic violence over the years, defecating in the corner of the sitting room.

Cairns (2002) and, more recently, Thomas and Philpot (2009) examine how foster care can be utilised to help traumatised children, who have been subject to abuse, recover. Increasingly such children make up most of the children placed in foster care. Thomas and Philpot, like Munro (2011), emphasise the importance of relationships, and argue that foster care is an art, not a science. They dismiss neither the importance of research findings informing foster care practice (indeed they draw on them to inform their positions) nor the need for regulation to govern foster care. Rather, in addition to research and regulation they posit that foster care involves dynamics that are less tangible:

> *It is the interplay between imagination and feelings that influences the outcome of fostering. Imaginative skill is a cornerstone of art and so, we would argue, fostering is the relationship between carers and the child and her interaction with the wider world.*

> (Thomas and Philpot, 2009, p33)

Goodyer's research (2011) involving interviews with 22 foster children from two local authorities is a welcome addition to the research findings about foster care informing SSW practice. She looks at her interview material from a sociology of childhood perspective, and argues for the need for a children's rights standpoint to be central to foster care and social work practice. Her work is valuable as it addresses the detail of children's experience, for example being moved between foster placements and the feelings of powerlessness that can provoke.

Although Thomas and Philpot's (2009) and Goodyer's (2011) arguments are informed by different theoretical influences, taken together what they have to say is valuable in informing SSW practice with foster carers to improve the care of and interaction with foster children. The Care Inquiry interestingly brings both together; the importance of foster children's relationships, including those with foster carers, and a children's rights perspective as follows:

> *The weight of evidence, from all quarters, convinces us that the relationships with people who care for and about children are the golden thread in children's lives, and that the quality of a child's relationships is the lens through which we should view what we do and plan to do. We have developed a set of recommendations that support this approach and that are consistent with the principles that underpin the United Nations Convention on the Rights of the Child and the Human Rights Act.*

> (Care Inquiry, 2013, p2)

To work well together and enable foster carers to deliver child-focused reparatory care to children, SSWs and foster carers have to build a working relationship of trust, openness and warmth, one within which they can manage conflict, and be straightforward with one another. As discussed in the previous chapter, the relationship between a fostering service and a foster carer starts from when the foster carer first applies to be assessed by that fostering service, and is developed through the assessment process. In cases where the assessment is done by a third party, not employed by the fostering service, it is sensible for there to be a handover, wherever possible, between the assessor and the social worker who will be supervising the foster carer, as indeed needs to happen even when the assessor is employed by the fostering service, when that person is not the one that has undertaken the assessment.

Face-to-face handovers enable relationship and information continuity, which is not just reliant on written records. For example, Gilligan (2009), examining the development of resilience in children in public care, emphasises the importance of those caring for children to believe in the possibility of change, a characteristic identified as important in Chapter 4, regarding assessment of prospective foster carers. In this regard helping a foster carer make the links between their own history, development and belief in the possibility of beneficial change, examined in their assessment to be a foster carer, with the supervisory material related to their care of foster children can be helpful. Making this link can develop the foster carer's empathy for a child, who might be provoking difficult emotions for them, and help them think strategically and practically about how to positively move forward.

I have argued in the previous chapter that foster carers need to believe in the possibility of change, be hopeful and have agency in the world; all these attributes will be drawn upon when helping foster children manage difficult feelings and related behaviour. Gilligan writes: *a resilience-led perspective tends to be optimistic and pragmatic. It believes that change is often possible, even in uncompromising conditions, and that change may start in simple ways; one thinks the glass is half full rather than half empty* (2009, p9). This approach fits with the ethos of the Fostering Changes and KEEP foster carer training programmes that many foster carers undertake in the UK, discussed in Chapter 6. As noted above, to be useful, the learning from such programmes has to be built upon in supervision to facilitate foster carers continuing to enact interventions that can help foster children change their behaviour. In other words, to be effective in making a difference to foster children's lives, foster carer development programmes' content, delivered through training, needs to be integrated into the content of ongoing supervision of foster carers, rather than being discreet entities that foster carers experience and benefit from, while on such programmes and immediately afterwards, but are unlikely to continue enacting the new learning unless integrated into ongoing supervision.

In Chapter 4, I listed the different 'types' of foster care as: emergency and short term; family and friends; multi-dimensional treatment foster care/intensive foster care; parent and child; permanent; remand; respite; short breaks; and support foster care. A foster child's placement, whichever 'type' of placement, will be part of that child's care plan, and what is required of their foster carer will be set out in the placement plan. The content of supervision therefore will vary, to some degree, according to the placement type. For example, in a parent and child placement, where a foster carer is responsible, in some part, for assessing the parent/child relationship, the quality of assessment skills and their recordings will be important to monitor in supervision, as well as the dynamics of having another adult in the household. In addition, the risk assessment aspects of caring for a young person on remand will be central to the supervisory process, along with the young person's overall well-being.

Working with the fostering family and their household

The fostering family

Lawson's components of supervision of foster carers includes the SSW *noting significant events and changes to the household* (2011b, p37). This is sometimes relatively straightforward, but can be an area of tension for SSWs and foster carers, involving, as it often does, the intimate details of a person's and foster family's life. This links directly to what is conveyed by Nutt's book title referred to above, *The Lives of Foster Carers: Private Sacrifices, Public Restrictions* (2006), and the public nature of foster care delivered in the once private space of the foster carer's home. For foster carers who have been recently approved it can take time to understand quite what is meant by the requirement to inform the fostering service of any changes to their household composition or to their circumstances, even though this will have been set out in their Foster Care Agreement (HM Government, 2011, p12). The details of this information might feel private, separate from them being foster carers, and not relevant to their care of foster children. For example, if a single, male foster carer forms a romantic attachment to a woman, where there is no plan for that woman to move into the fostering household, or if a foster carer's 27-year-old son, living with his partner five miles from the foster home, is arrested for theft, both fostering households may not see this information as relevant to their fostering.

To have new private matters discussed and recorded can feel intrusive, unless it is elicited in a sensitive manner and the purpose of the need to have such information is clear to the foster carer. What happens to a foster carer and their family does impact on their fostering, because it will in turn impinge on their emotional life and often on practical arrangements, and both could affect their care of foster children. The actual change or new development in a foster carer's life might not in itself be problematic, but it will need to be explored with the SSW, and if there are associated foster care related difficulties that arise, how those difficulties can be mitigated will need to be thought about. However, in some cases the nature of a foster carer's change of circumstance or new composition of their household might mean that they can no longer foster.

A recurrent theme in social work is our seeming reluctance to engage with men in social work undertaken with families (Featherstone, 2010). The person perceived as the primary carer is usually the focus of a social worker's attention and intervention; this is also common practice in foster care. In most cases where heterosexual couples foster, SSWs usually see more of the female carer and much less of the male foster carer. However, if a couple are approved as foster carers, irrespective of their gender or sexual orientation, both parties of the couple need to be engaged in supervision, as both are responsible for the foster care of children placed with them. In addition, the dynamics of their relationship will influence the quality of the foster care provided. Realistically not every supervision session will be with both members of a fostering couple, but to make sure that foster children thrive in a fostering placement both need to engage in most supervision sessions.

The foster home

Another area that we as social workers have been found to be remiss is how we use physical movement as part of our practice. Ferguson (2010), writing about child protection practice, but equally relevant to foster care, writes about the importance of engaging with, and being present in, all parts of the home, and the intimate aspects of family life to ensure children's welfare.

SSWs have to be familiar with every part of a foster carer's home, as part of their responsibility to *manage risk, health and safety and ensuring safer care* (Lawson, 2011b, p37). They are also required to make judgements about the condition of a foster home, for example, is it clean enough? Is it modelling organised family life? Is the foster child's bedroom comfortable, age appropriate and personalised? If they think an area is lacking, SSWs need professional confidence to engage sensitively, proactively, warmly and with clarity regarding the practical realisable detail of how things can be improved. Given the intimate family home nature of foster care, this can involve difficult subjects such as a smelly loo.

Foster carers' children

Engaging with the fostering family involves holding foster carers' children in mind. The research findings suggest that fostering does impinge on foster carers' children's lives, as they do in turn on the success of a placement (Wilson *et al.*, 2004). Foster carers' children are not just birth children, but sometimes include adopted children, and children subject to Special Guardianship Orders and Residence Orders, and might have significant needs of their own. For social workers to engage meaningfully with children in the foster home they have to feel comfortable communicating with and relating to children for that contact to be purposeful (Luckock and Lefevre, 2008; Lefevre, 2010). Much excellent work is done with foster carers' children by SSWs and fostering services, and some of the best is where the fostering service makes available such things as prizes, outings and awards equally to foster children and foster carers' children.

There are some problematic dynamics that fostering services themselves introduce inadvertently into a fostering family that have to be managed carefully. For example, foster children are sometimes required by the fostering service to have a specific amount of pocket money, or sum of money spent on their birthday. For some fostering families the amounts involved are more than they could afford to give their children, thus introducing a potential dynamic of jealousy, which the SSW needs to work with so the fostering family's children feel cared for and held in mind.

Positive foster care is when a foster carer makes no unnecessary distinction between their foster child and their own. Indeed the Regulations and Guidance suggest that: *the default position should be that the foster carer does not treat the child differently from their own children* (HM Government, 2011, p12). However, this can pose difficulties for foster carers and SSWs when the corporate parent for the foster child and those who hold parental responsibility have different ideas about a specific decision, for example, whether or not a five-year-old disabled boy should have riding lessons.

Placement planning

Matching is an important variable related to the success of a fostering placement. However, many placements are made at short notice in an emergency, and often in such cases 'matching' is not a consideration. For permanent placements, or where a placement lasts for longer than was planned, the match between a foster carer and a child has been shown to be important (Schofield, Beek and Ward, 2012). Boddy (2013), in her review of the literature on permanence, points out that there are many components to 'matching', including the expectations of a child and a fostering family.

For a successful placement to be possible a careful assessment of the foster child needs to take place, and the findings of that assessment matched with the family composition, attributes, history, skills and emotional and intellectual capacity of a foster carer. Lawson identifies pertinent areas relating to information about the child, the foster carer and the plan for the placement, which act as useful prompts for a child's social worker and SSW when matching a foster child with a foster family (2011b, p51).

Matching is rarely about one foster child and a particular foster carer, but rather involves thinking also about the other foster children that a foster carer might already have placed with them. Having too many unrelated foster children placed with a fostering family can result in a foster carer being unable to meet all the associated emotional and practical requirements for each of their foster children, for example school runs and contact arrangements. In addition too many children being placed with a foster carer can mean that the emotional needs of foster children are too great or too various to realistically be met by a single foster carer or a fostering couple. Placing too many needy foster children with foster carers can result in a disruption to a foster child's placement. Over-stretching foster carers is a short-sighted and, in the long term, expensive approach. All placement decisions for foster children need to be carefully considered to make sure that a foster carer will be able to meet the emotional needs of all the foster children placed with them, as well as the practicalities of each of the placements identified in their placement and care plan.

Placement planning meetings, placement plans and delegated authority

One vehicle for making sure that all those responsible for the realisation of a foster child's care plan are clear about their roles and responsibilities is through the placement planning meeting where the placement plan is agreed; this is arranged and chaired by the foster child's social worker (Dibben, 2012). The placement plan should be devised and agreed within five working days of the start of the placement (HM Government, 2010; Department of Education, 2013c), if it has not been possible to hold the meeting prior to the foster child being placed. It is the expectation of the Department of Education that the placement planning meeting is where delegated authority is discussed, agreed and recorded as part of the placement plan (Department of Education, 2013c). Many fostering services and local authorities use the Department of Education/Fostering Network Guidance and paperwork to facilitate this process.

> *It is important that foster carers know what authority they have to make decisions about everyday matters involving the child. Arrangements for delegating authority from the parents to the local authority, and/or from the local authority to the foster carers, must be discussed and agreed as part of the care planning process, particularly at placement planning meetings, and agreements should be recorded in the placement plan.*

> (HM Government, 2011, p16)

The intention behind delegated authority is that foster children should have as ordinary a childhood as is possible, and that they are not singled out as different from their peers, when this is not necessary. The foster child's social worker has to work with the person, or people with parental responsibility, engaging them in the delegated responsibility process and, wherever possible, and in the child's interests, for them to be part of the placement planning meeting. The SSW's role is pivotal in the placement planning meeting to make sure that the foster carer is an active participant as described in Standard 31.1 of the NMS: *the fostering service supports foster carers to play an active role in agreeing the contents of each child's placement plan, in conjunction with the responsible authority* (Department of Education, 2011a, p60). The placement planning meeting is where the detail of the placement is agreed and the requirements placed on the foster carer identified; for example, how a particular behaviour will be managed, taking a child to school, to contact, giving medication, etc. Lawson argues that:

> *Supervising and children's social workers need to be confident about discuss-*
> *ing parental responsibility and delegated authority to enable foster carers to*
> *play an informed and proactive role in care planning, as well as in day-to-day*
> *decision-making.*

> (Lawson, 2011b, p73)

As noted earlier many placements start before the placement planning meeting happens, and sometimes the placing social worker or police officer has limited information about the child. This means that the SSW and foster carer need to think together in supervision about how to welcome foster children, in general, so that a foster carer can then apply some of that general thinking to a particular foster child. This supervisory work can help a foster carer articulate the culture, day-to-day functioning and dynamics of their family household, and imagine how that might be experienced by a child coming to live with them. In addition the SSW and foster carer have to plan how to enable a child, who has experienced recent, often traumatic, separation from their birth family, or another foster placement, or residential placement, feel as at ease as possible, in the circumstances, in their new foster home. Welcoming a foster child is a complex task, to be thought about carefully.

Team around the child

The foster carer and SSW are part of the team around the child, responsible for the realisation of the foster child's care plan incorporating their placement plan. This necessitates both the SSW and the foster carer working effectively with other professionals to make sure that the multi-professional team works effectively to meet the foster child's emotional, physical and mental health needs, and educational potential.

Being part of this multi-professional team involving health, education and social services, and sometimes legal professionals, Youth Offending Services and others, means that the foster carer has to manage the bureaucratic aspects of their role efficiently. For example, attending and being effective in meetings, and keeping required records in the format expected by their fostering service. Foster carers are expected to be proactive in relation to a child's education, supporting them at home as well as liaising closely with their school, and regarding their physical and mental health. Some foster children will need Children and Adolescent Mental Health Service interventions, and foster carers might themselves be part of the work that is done. SSWs have to support foster carers with their involvement with such services, to make sure that their foster child benefits.

Professionalisation of foster carers

One of the consequences of what is described as the professionalisation of foster care, taken forward by Care Matters (Department for Education and Skills, 2007), has been the raised expectations placed on foster carers as members of the multi-professional team around the child. This comes to the fore in two areas: first, training and development, and second, recording. The first will be considered in Chapter 6. In respect of the second, increasingly fostering services want foster carers to record electronically and this can be a source of anxiety for those who are not confident using computers. Where this is the case the SSW and the foster carer need to identify this as an area of development to be recorded in their annual review of the foster carer's PDP. Foster carer recording is crucial as it provides evidence of their foster care, and the development, well-being and circumstances of their foster child.

SSWs and foster children's social workers' child-focused communication

One of the roles of an SSW is to be the conduit for support for foster carers. Lawson writes:

> *Since supervising social workers are responsible for overseeing the support pro-*
> *vided for foster carers, this will be a major focus of their supervisory visits and*
> *also of any review of the foster carer's approval. Support will be required form*
> *the child's social worker and a range of other agencies and professionals, as well*
> *as from the supervising social worker themselves, and so they need to keep up*
> *to date about the adequacy of support offered and should follow up anything*
> *that is lacking.*

(Lawson, 2011b, p33)

To be a successful conduit requires the SSW to communicate effectively with the foster child's social worker, ensuring that they are child-focused and working together in respect of the foster child's care plan, health needs, education and contact arrangements.

The child has to be central to their care plan, an odd thing to write given that is self-evident. However, Goodyer's (2011) work indicated that foster children did not always feel that to be the case. Foster children's wishes and feelings need to be elicited to inform both their own children looked after reviews, and their foster carers' reviews. A young person's quote at the end of the Care Inquiry report (2013) is a helpful reminder of the importance of hearing what children and young people say:

> *I've been in care since I was six and one of the things that really bugged me and*
> *annoyed me about social workers is that they think they know how you feel and*
> *they say 'I know what you're going through' but they don't know what you're*
> *feeling. I think that everyone needs to listen properly to children and not make*
> *assumptions.*

(Care Inquiry, 2013, p24)

Foster carer and fostering service communication

A foster carer's ability to work well with their SSW and with the fostering service is central to safe and helpful foster care. This requires them to communicate regularly and respond to contact made with them by their SSW in a timely manner. When there are difficulties in this regard these need to be addressed quickly and explicitly in supervision. One area of communication difficulty that can arise relates to holidays and respite for foster carers. Some fostering services plan respite breaks for their foster carers, others do not. Holidays can be a cause of tension between foster carers, the child's social worker and the SSW. *The default position should be that the foster carer does not treat the child differently from their own children* (HM Government, 2011, p12). In line with this guidance the expectation is that a fostering family will usually take a foster child away on holiday with them; as indeed many do. However, this does not always happen. In some cases it might be agreed by the child's social worker and the fostering service that to maintain the stability of the placement the foster child and foster family need some planned time apart, because of the particular difficulties that they might be experiencing. Otherwise, when holidays are taken by a foster family without a foster child they have to be planned well in advance, wherever possible, to enable the foster child to be either cared for within the foster carer's home by a known person, usually under delegated authority, or arrangements made for them to stay with another foster family or with their birth family, when this is agreed.

Foster carers and their support networks

Working well with others involves the foster carer communicating effectively with their support network, whom the fostering service has agreed can step in to help with the care of a foster child if, and when, needed. Part of an SSW's role is to make sure that a foster carer has such a support network, to lessen any potential disruption to a foster child if an unforeseen circumstance arose. Reviewing a foster carer support network should be part of what is considered at regular intervals in supervision, and at the foster carer's review.

Working effectively with others involved with and responsible for a foster child means also working with a child's birth family, and others that are significant to them, when this is part of the placement and care plan.

Contact

Foster carers can feel that they take the brunt of some of the dynamics associated with contact, and need to be helped by their SSWs and their foster child's social worker to understand the importance of contact for children. However, foster carers also have important things to say about the impact contact has on their foster child, and are able to feed their observations into the review of a child looked after, and to alert the child's social worker where there are particular difficulties.

Wilson *et al.* (2004) note the conflicting findings regarding contact and its benefit for foster children, but posit that *the present position appears to be that there is a strong official presumption in favour of contact and this is accepted by social workers and with some reservations by foster carers* (2004, p46). Foster carers who care for foster children every day, and often know them better than the other professionals involved, can benefit from contact being a regular agenda item in supervision, to make sure that they and others are focusing on what is best for their foster child. Austerberry, Stanley, Larkins, Ridley, Farrelly, Manthorpe and Hussein's study looking at contact and the support foster carers received from a child's social worker found that 68 per cent of their sample wanted help in managing contact (2013, p120). Boddy (2013) reminds us that the increased use of social media makes managing contact with birth families considerably more complex than it was 20 years ago.

The purpose of contact is defined by Adams as:

> (1) *enabling attachment to new carers (by countering feelings of guilt, anxiety and self-blame, and by avoiding idealisation);*
>
> (2) *promoting positive identity (by providing the child with genealogical and historical information);*
>
> (3) *enabling emotional healing and promoting self-esteem (by dealing with loss, trauma and rejection).*

(Adams, 2012, p10)

Often contact is not only about contact with parents, but includes contact with siblings and sometimes previous carers, and other significant people for a foster child. Wilson and Sinclair (2004) note the importance of identifying the purpose of contact for a specific foster child, and how this is likely to differ for children who are placed permanently with a foster carer, from those where the plan is that they return to their birth family, and from a child who is subject to care proceedings and the outcome of those proceedings is still unknown.

Foster children moving on

Foster children move from a foster family, in a planned way, for a variety of reasons, including when a decision has been made that the child moves back to their birth family; or to family and friends foster carers; or to another foster carer who can offer a permanent placement; or to an adoptive family or a special guardianship placement. In each of these scenarios the foster carer will work with whoever is going to care for the foster child, to make sure that the child experiences as smooth a transition as possible.

Foster carers usually undertake the introduction plan for a foster child with their prospective permanent family, within their own home over a one- to two-week period. This introduction work requires empathy and sensitivity, on the part of the foster carer as well as communication skills to enable the prospective carer and foster child to start to form a relationship, and for the prospective carer to gradually take over the care of the foster child. Given that most of this work is done within the foster carer's own home, often with a foster child that the foster carer has formed an enabling attachment to, this is a complex piece of work, one which the foster carer should be supported in undertaking by their SSW, and the child's social worker. Capable foster carers have the emotional capacity to manage this work in such a way that gives a solid start to the prospective carer's relationship with the child.

Foster carers who have the ability to love their foster child, thus enabling them to develop well in their care, and help the child move on, often feel great sadness when their foster child leaves, at the same time as feeling happy for them that they have been found a permanent family. At such times SSWs need to support their foster carer to talk about the experience, and help them manage the loss of that foster child, in readiness to start again, caring for another foster child.

Some placement endings are not planned, and these endings can be damaging for foster children and foster carers alike. Argent and Coleman's book about disruptions in fostering and adoption placements is particularly useful for social workers and foster carers, as it gives an overview of research findings concerning disruptions, and looks at the practice and processes involved. I have selected, from their identified common causes of disruption, ones relevant to foster care as follows:

> *Key information is incomplete or unshared; inaccurate assessments of children's attachment patterns; changes in the family; failure of therapeutic, health and education services; poor inter-agency and inter-departmental communication; not enough support; an adult agenda rather than a child-centred introduction plan; not enough consideration of carer's own children's needs and perspectives; lack of clarity and agreement about both the purpose and management of contact; inadequate placement support; not enough preparation of a child or children for the move to permanence; not enough preparation of the prospective carers to parent this particular child or sibling group.*
>
> (Argent and Coleman, 2012, pp18–22)

We can see from this list that some of these causes could be mitigated by the proactive work of the SSW and child's social worker to enhance the possibility of maintaining stability for a foster child.

Managing allegations

All foster carers need safer care agreements for each foster child they care for, incorporating the general expectations of the fostering service regarding such things as behaviour management, as well as being specific to the individual child, so that all involved agree what is expected. Caring for troubled, traumatised children can pose dilemmas for foster carers in how they manage risk, and keep children safe (Cairns and Fursland, 2007; Slade, 2012). Each foster child needs to have a safer care agreement that is specific to them, and enables calculated risk taking for them to have as ordinary an experience of family life as possible. SSWs and foster carers are key in devising these safer care agreements, in consultation with the child's social worker.

For foster children and foster carers to be as 'safe' as possible, a combination of a well-thought-out safer care agreement and placement plan, where delegated authority is clearly established, can help to clarify for everyone, parents, the child's social worker, the foster carer, all those in the fostering household and the SSW, what is expected.

However, even with the best-made plans sometimes things go wrong, and allegations are made against foster carers. In such cases an efficient and effective response by the fostering service can help to lessen the trauma experienced by all concerned. A close working relationship between the child's social worker and the SSW enables a planned, co-ordinated and timely response. SSWs need to be familiar with the findings of the Wakefield Inquiry (Parrott *et al.*, 2007) relating to the importance of the effective working relationship between the SSW and the child's social worker, and the SSW remaining open to the possibility that a foster carer might not be offering the good quality foster care that they should. Supervision of foster carers does involve a significant support element, as noted above, because to enable a foster carer to care well for a foster child the foster carer needs to feel cared for themselves, by the fostering service and their SSW. Making sure foster carers are supported, understood and treated as fellow professionals can sit comfortably with assertive and rigorous supervision.

Allegations against foster carers provoke powerful feelings for foster carers, SSWs and foster children's social workers. It is common for these 'powerful feelings' to contribute to professionals involved taking up certain and fixed positions (Munro, 2008), and as a result not working closely or openly with others responsible for the foster child.

The prevalence of substantiated maltreatment by foster carers of foster children in the UK is unclear (Biehal, 2013). In Biehal and Parry's review of the evidence of maltreatment and allegations of maltreatment in foster care, they conclude that there are only a few studies that tell us a little.

> It is difficult to come to clear conclusions about the extent of these problems. However, evidence from two UK studies suggests that around 3.5 to five per cent of foster carers in the UK may experience allegations of abuse in a single year and that confirmed maltreatment may be found in relation to less than one per cent of foster carers per annum. According to another UK study, 16 per cent may have experienced allegations at some point during the course of their fostering careers (although this figure refers only to practising carers and excludes those who may have given up fostering or been de-registered as a consequence of an allegation). How many children experience confirmed maltreatment over the entire period of time that they have lived in foster care is even harder to quantify, as estimates of the prevalence of maltreatment range from three to 19 per cent of children in foster care.
>
> (Biehal and Parry, 2010, p41)

What the Standards, Guidance and Regulations say regarding allegations

The Guidance on managing allegations is to be found in:

- The Children Act 1989 Guidance and Regulations Volume 4: Fostering Services (HM Government, 2011, pp25–7, Section 3.68);

- The NMS (Department of Education, 2011a, pp44–6, Standard 22);

- Working Together to Safeguard Children: A guide to inter-agency working to safeguard and promote the welfare of children (HM Government, 2013b).

Allegations have to be thoroughly and rigorously investigated, and the NMS dictate that fostering services need to make sure that: *Investigations into allegations or suspicions of harm are handled fairly, quickly, and consistently in a way that provides effective protection for the child, and at the same time supports the person who is the subject of the allegation* (Department of Education, 2011a, p45). All allegations have to be taken seriously, however unlikely they may seem to those involved. The SSW in the Wakefield case (Parrott *et al.*, 2007) did not think that the foster carers involved were of concern, and as a result the fostering team did not take seriously worries being raised by the foster children's social workers, or by one of the foster children's mothers. Eunice Spry was assessed as a foster carer, and an adopter, and despite concerns being raised about her parenting on 12 separate occasions she cared for other people's children for 20 years before eventually receiving a custodial sentence for child neglect and abuse (Gloucestershire Safeguarding Children Board, 2008). It is an exceptionally rare occurrence, but some foster carers do occasionally harm children, and in some extreme cases kill children.

Investigating allegations

Most allegations fall into the murky area between needing to involve the Local Authority Designated Officer (LADO), because it is a matter of, or a potential matter of, significant harm (HM Government, 2013b), and a standard of care matter. In practice the overlap between the two can be difficult to disentangle. The Guidance notes that sometimes allegations are false: . . . *foster carers do face a risk of being the subject of false allegations and this can be extremely traumatic for those involved and their families* (HM Government, 2011, p25). As noted in Chapter 3 it is understandable that a foster child or a parent might make a false allegation for a variety of reasons, sometimes in the belief, or hope, that it will mean that a child might be returned to their family.

The LADO's involvement happens when there is an allegation that falls into the 'significant harm' category. The Guidance notes:

> *The Fostering Service must make a clear distinction between investigations into allegations of harm and discussions over standard of care. An investigation which finds no evidence of harm should not become a procedure to look into poor standards of care, which should be addressed separately.*

> (HM Government, 2011, p26)

Fostering services will have guidelines congruent with Working Together to Safeguard Children (HM Government, 2013b), setting out the procedures regarding how allegations are managed. The SSW and the fostering service need to make sure that foster carers are aware of the processes involved if and when an allegation is made or standard of care matter raised. During an investigation of an allegation or standard of care matter, the continuing child-focused working relationship between the SSW and the child's social worker helps to safeguard children, and make sure that foster carers are treated fairly. The foster carer should be told by their SSW/fostering service how they can secure the support of an independent advocate (Department of Education, 2011a, p46). Clarity, timeliness and openness will enhance good working relationships between the fostering service, the SSW, the foster child's social worker and the foster carer, even though the investigation process is often experienced by those involved as traumatic. Where there has been an allegation made, involving the LADO, or standard of care matter raised, in both instances it is best practice for a foster carer review to subsequently be held (Borthwick and Lord, 2011).

Valuing and developing a child's heritage/positive sense of self

Fundamental to capable foster care is the ability to help a child maintain and develop a strong, positive sense of who they are. This is not an easy task given that many children will have entered the care system with fragmented senses of who they are, resulting from the neglect and/or abuse/dislocation/separation they might have experienced. To build their resilience and positive self-regard is one of the responsibilities of foster carers, SSWs and the child's social worker, to enhance their well-being. Foster carers do this work with the help of others from: a foster carer's community; school/college; health; and sport, creative and leisure organisations. Foster carers can act as a safe bridge for foster children, helping them make productive links with others to strengthen their positive experiences of the world and themselves. For example, a young man of 15 years of age who is currently excluded from school being taken by their foster carer every Saturday to play rugby at a local club can be helpful. Even though the young person ostensibly says it is embarrassing that his foster carer stands on the sideline screaming herself hoarse in support of him, this makes a positive difference to his feelings about exclusion and failure.

As noted in Chapter 4 many placements of children with foster carers will not be a 'match' regarding their religion, ethnicity or national heritage; some will be, but many will not. For black and ethnic minority children placed with white foster carers who live in predominately white areas, the SSW needs to consider in detail and depth with the foster carer how that foster child can be helped to feel they belong in the family and community, and keep their black and ethnic minority identity alive and flourishing. As noted previously to 'match' some children would be difficult, given the richness of their ethnic heritages, sometimes representing many ethnicities and nationalities. In such cases SSWs need to actively engage with foster carers in supervision about how the foster carer enacts respecting, valuing and keeping alive that child's heritage. To do this foster carers have to be active, curious and confident to explore cultures, religions and nationalities that may not be familiar to them. They need passionate curiosity to engage with their foster child in this exploration, in a sensitive and optimistic manner. I write this because foster children can have negative associations with aspects of their heritage, because it can be linked in their mind to abuse or trauma they experienced. For example, a mixed-heritage child whose French grandfather emotionally abused them might be dismissive of their French heritage, preferring to explore their Irish and Pakistani lineage instead.

Sometimes discussions about keeping a child's heritage alive can be reductionist in nature, with culture being associated just with food, clothes and religious observance. However, even here a foster carer trying their best to cook a Nigerian dish, with their Nigerian foster child, conveys to that child their motivation to engage with who that child is, their heritage and in many cases their ongoing family relationships. What makes a difference to the meaning of such activities, for those involved, is not the activity in itself but the spirit in which it is engaged.

The research findings regarding how children fare placed within families who have a different ethnic, religious and cultural heritage from their own have been predominantly focused on adoption. Although there are similarities, there are also significant differences in that foster children are more likely to maintain regular face-to-face contact with their families; will in some case return home; and the legal link with their family has not been severed, as is the case in adoption. Sinclair, reviewing the existing research findings in 2005 noted: *ethnic minority children placed with carers from ethnic minorities were no more or less likely to have a placement breakdown than similar children placed with a white family* (2005, p73). Caballero, Edwards, Goodyer and Okitikpi in their 2012 paper argue for moving on from the traditional 'colour blind', 'same-race', 'pragmatic' social care paradigms related to debates in this area of child welfare, to an appreciation of ordinariness. Drawing on my own practice experience as an independent reviewing officer chairing foster carers' reviews this makes sense. I review foster carers from diverse ethnic, cultural and religious heritages who care for children from as diverse backgrounds as themselves. Sometimes there is a 'match', but often there is not. The striking message from the foster carers is that they experience caring for children from a range of different backgrounds as 'ordinary', the same message articulated by the mixed racial and ethnic families in Caballero *et al.*'s study. When it works well this ordinariness, in the case of foster care, is not 'colour blind' or merely 'pragmatic' but incorporates an understanding of the complexity of a child's sense of their ethnicity, culture and religion, where that is relevant, and the need to proactively enact respect, valuing and interest, to help a child gain a stronger sense of who they are, their history and heritage at the same time as appreciating what is shared in common.

Some foster children are placed in what might be referred to as matched placements, when the foster carer and child are assumed to share the same cultural, religious and ethnic heritage. However, we know how different each family is, and how disorientating it can feel when something that should be familiar is experienced as different. Each family is unique and an SSW needs to help a foster family include a child by helping them contribute to how they and their foster family undertake particular activities. For example, a Polish foster family caring for a Polish child could consider how they incorporate their foster child's family's way of preparing for Saint Nicholas bringing presents to children on the night of 6 December into their own traditions. The foster family adjusting their behaviour and incorporating the expectations of the foster child, at the same time as respecting the foster family's own children's traditions, can help that foster child feel valued and included.

Placement story work

The foster carer, their friends and family will contribute to a child's experience, and become part of their history. Foster carers with the support of their SSWs have to maintain and regularly update the foster child's placement story, which becomes part of their life story work. As well as labelled photographs, which include the detail of people, where they were and what they were doing at the time, the collection of objects is also significant. The stone collected on a beach, the first time the foster child saw the sea at Whitstable, the pink fluffy bunny rabbit they won at the local fair, long since forgotten now they are 14 years of age, but fundamentally important to them when they are 32 years old talking to their own child about their childhood, need to be treasured and kept carefully for the future by their foster carer.

Caring for 'separated', unaccompanied asylum-seeking children and young people

All foster children and young people have experienced dislocation in that they are separated from their families. Separated children and young people seeking asylum in the UK experience dislocation in many ways. Foster carers for such young people can help them by creating a safe space and acting as a bridge between the foster family where they are placed and the community and authorities they will encounter. Wade, Sirriyeh, Kohli and Simmonds' study, examining the foster care of separated, unaccompanied asylum-seeking young people, included looking at how SSWs help foster carers *create a family life across a world of differences* (2012). Their study's findings regarding the SSW role are broader than just those relating to their care of separated, unaccompanied asylum-seeking young people. For example, they looked at foster carers' perceptions of the overall quality of the support given to foster carers by SSWs.

> *Our interviews with foster carers also highlighted the high quality of relationships that had often been forged with supervising social workers, emphasising their availability, responsiveness and, in some instances, their place within the fabric of family life.*

(Wade *et al.*, 2012, p267)

Caring for disabled children and young people

Facilitating a child or young person to develop a positive view of themselves, and agency in the world, is particularly relevant for foster carers who foster children with physical disabilities and learning disabilities. Peake's (2009) study found that many foster carers caring for disabled children felt ill prepared. The NMS (Department of Education, 2011a) requires fostering services to adequately prepare foster carers to meet the needs of children with complex needs. Lawson (2011b) reminds us that disabled children are not a homogenous group, and have abilities, skills and interests to be developed and nurtured and ones still to be built. Their unique individuality has to be recognised by the foster carer and their SSW, to safeguard against their disability taking precedence, and becoming the sole social work focus.

Caring for young lesbians and gay men

Despite fundamental changes to the position of lesbians and gay men in the UK in the last 20 years (Brown and Kershaw, 2008), some young lesbians and gay men remain vulnerable. Undoubtedly a number of young lesbians and gay men experience difficulty associated with how others perceive their sexual orientation (Forsyth, 2000; Gold, 2005; Guasp, 2012; Brown, forthcoming). They might experience problems in care, in education, with their mental health and in their housing status. However, as Daniel writes, *focusing on them only as powerless victims may not be the most helpful approach* (2008, p91).

Recruiting, assessing, supervising and supporting foster carers who are able to meet the emotional, social, health and educational needs of young lesbians and gay men is part of a local authority's corporate parenting responsibilities. Some young people will come out as lesbian or gay in foster placements where they have lived for many years, and others will come into care as young people who already identify as lesbian or gay. Brown and Cocker (2011) write about the need for social workers to acknowledge the complex dynamics in foster placements, when a young person comes out, and the importance of working proactively, and empathetically with both the foster carer and the young person, to make sure that the placement is not disrupted because of the foster carers' reaction to the young person's sexuality, so that bonds of affection and continuity can be maintained. SSWs have a clear supervisory role in such cases to help maintain the stability of a young person's placement, when it is in the fostered young person's interests.

Permanence

Emergency, short-term or permanent fostering placement categories are rarely clear cut. The emphasis on permanence for children who are looked after, central to the Care Matters White Paper agenda (Department for Education and Skills, 2007), was reiterated in the Care Inquiry (2013). Where possible, to avoid unnecessary moves for a child, placements that were 'short term' at the time they were made are being made into permanent placements where the foster child is thriving, and decisions have been made meaning the child cannot return to their birth family's care. In cases where permanence with a foster child's fostering family is being considered, foster carers need supervision and support from their SSWs, and the child's social worker, to consider the serious long-term implications of caring for a child as a permanent member of their family.

Permanent foster care has different implications for foster carers and their families from short-term foster care, and needs careful thought. It is undoubtedly in a foster child's interest to remain with their foster carer, if that placement is helping them develop and thrive, but it would not be in their interest for that same placement to disrupt six years after the permanence decision had been made, because the foster carer found it too hard to care for a challenging fifteen year old, who had been a compliant nine year old when first placed with them. Boddy's recent review of the research findings relating to permanence (2013) can helpfully inform social workers when undertaking this work with foster carers and their families.

Chapter summary

- The jury remains out in respect of research findings that definitively inform us about whether or not the quantity, and quality, of supervision and support to foster carers makes a difference to foster children's lives.

- We do know it makes a difference to the retention of foster carers, and given the shortage of foster carers this is significant.

- Despite the ambiguous research findings I have argued, like Lawson (2011b), that the supervision and support of foster carers can make a difference to the quality of foster care for an individual foster child, and that supervision is a core component of the overall quality assurance of foster care.

FURTHER READING

Wilson, K, Sinclair, I, Taylor, C, Pithouse, A and Sellick, C (2004) *Fostering Success: An Exploration of the Research Literature in Foster Care*. Knowledge Review 5. London: Social Care Institute for Excellence/ Bristol: Policy Press.

Sellick, C, Thoburn, J and Philpot, T (2004) *What Works in Adoption and Foster Care?* Barkingside: Barnardo's.

Sinclair, I (2005) *Fostering Now: Messages from Research*. London: Jessica Kingsley Publishers.

Boddy, J (2013) *Understanding Permanence for Looked After Children: A Review of Research for the Care Inquiry*. London: Nuffield Foundation.

The above literature reviews provide a useful summary of the research evidence available about foster care in general.

Schofield, G and Simmonds, J (eds) (2009) *The Child Placement Handbook: Research, Policy and Practice*. London: British Association for Adoption and Fostering.

This book gives an overview of various aspects of foster care.

Lawson, D (2011b) *A Foster Care Handbook for Supervising Social Workers (England)*. London: The Fostering Network.

Lawson's book on the role of the SSW is currently the only one of its kind and links the role to the current legal and policy framework for foster care.

Chapter 6

Foster carer development and training

CHAPTER OBJECTIVES

By the end of this chapter, readers should:

- be familiar with the regulatory requirements regarding foster carer training and development;
- understand what the research tells us about the effectiveness of different sorts of foster carer training;
- appreciate how we might use the knowledge available to us about foster carer training and development, to enhance our work with foster carers regarding their personal development plans and supervision.

Introduction

The placement of children in foster care can be, at its worst, just a 'holding operation' until a child is placed back home with his or her birth family, placed with a family and friends foster carer, placed in residential care or placed with a permanent substitute family through adoption, special guardianship, a residence order or permanent foster care. Minimalist expectations of foster care deliver minimal beneficial outcomes for children. To enable foster care to be a purposeful and beneficial intervention in children's lives fostering services have to develop and support their foster carers, and their social workers, to deliver the best quality foster care possible.

As noted earlier in the book the importance of foster care was recognised by the Government in 2007 within the White Paper Care Matters (Department for Education and Skills, 2007), and again in 2012 when the Department of Education declared the Government's intention to improve fostering services (Loughton, 2012). Both initiatives emphasised the need to raise the status of foster care through a number of mechanisms, including foster carer support, development and training. This focus on foster care was related to concern about the number of moves foster children experience once in the care system, and the need to improve both the quality of foster care and the stability children in public care experience. *A successful, stable placement is central to supporting the needs of children in care. Carers are the centre of a child's or young person's experience of corporate parenting and should provide the mainstay of their support* (Department for Education and Skills, 2007, p8). Foster care should provide a safe, containing, stimulating and caring experience of family life for a child. As noted in Chapter 5 it can also be an effective reparatory family intervention, improving the chances for foster children by mitigating the effects of past damaging experiences, and thus helping children fulfil their potential.

As noted in the last chapter, the SSW has a responsibility to help develop a foster carer's competence and skills (HM Government, 2011, p43). The identification of areas of development comes about through the SSW working with the foster carer to formulate their personal development plan (PDP), which is reviewed annually. Foster carer development happens via a range of methods including: foster carer's own reading and initiatives; SSW supervision and support, covered in the previous chapter; fostering services' training; and foster carer mutual support via either support groups or individual mentoring.

Joint training between foster carers, members of the fostering service's fostering panel, foster children's social workers and SSWs has the potential to enhance joint understanding of the subject under discussion, and increase effective communication between different groups who are responsible for foster children. Joint training also symbolises all parts of the fostering service working together in the interests of foster children. Such training usefully includes areas relevant to all parties such as: delegated authority; placement planning meetings and placement plans; foster carer reviews; enhancing the educational attainment of foster children; meeting the physical and mental health needs of children; planning for transitions; helping young people move on to independence; allegations and standards of care; and contact with foster children's families.

This chapter covers

- The Skills to Foster preparation training programme

- Personal development plans (PDPs)

- The Training Support and Development Standards (TSDS)

- What the research tells us about the effectiveness of training for foster carers

- Fostering Changes

- Multidimensional Treatment Foster Care (MTFC)/Keeping Foster Parents Trained and Supported, KEEP

- Foster carer support groups.

The Skills to Foster training programme

The NMS Standard 20, 'Learning and Development of Foster Carers', places a requirement on fostering services to ensure that *foster carers receive the training and development they need to carry out their role effectively* (Department of Education, 2011a, p40). This includes making sure that foster carers are adequately equipped once they are approved as foster carers, to take on their first placement of a foster child. Foster carers have to be prepared through training and induction for the role of foster carer. Local authorities and independent fostering agencies have, for some time, as part of the assessment process for prospective foster carers, run the Skills to Foster programme (The Fostering Network, 2009). This training programme is designed to prepare foster carers to foster. The programme covers seven areas as follows: what do foster carers do; identity and life chances; working with others; understanding children in foster care; safer caring; transitions; and my family fosters (The Fostering Network, 2009).

The social work assessor, and the prospective foster carer, during the foster carer's assessment record, in the assessment report, future training they think should be undertaken to help the foster carer be effective. This identified training is then built upon, and included by the foster carer's SSW within the formulation of the foster carer's initial PDP.

Personal development plans (PDPs)

It is the responsibility of the SSW to create and record a personal development plan (PDP) with each of their foster carers, which is then reviewed annually at the foster carer's review (Department of Education, 2012b). This personal development plan is likely to include training, as noted above, to enable the foster carer's development. For all foster carers, once approved by their fostering service, the PDP should include the foster carer's necessary completion of the Department of Education's TSDS (Department of Education, 2012b).

For a meaningful PDP to be devised work is required by the foster carer and their SSW, so that each PDP is personalised, and tailor-made to meet the development needs of the specific foster carer. The PDP will not just identify training thought to be useful to the foster carer's development, but in addition will cover areas to be focused on in supervision, and actions and development initiatives that the foster carer themselves will take on. For example, in relation to the acquisition of fluent spoken and written English, a foster carer might identify the need to develop their language skills themselves, and enrol on a relevant course at a local college. Some foster carers need both spoken and written English language support, because a number of foster carers have other languages, rather than English, as their first language. For others whose first language is English, their written English skills might not be at the level that will be required of them to fulfil what is expected by their fostering service, regarding written records and the keeping of financial accounts. In addition there are foster carers who need support in making the transition from hand-written to electronic recording. Identifying the need for support for spoken and written English and electronic recording can be a sensitive area for foster carers, and one that has to be approached empathetically, sensitively and purposefully to enable an individual foster carer to develop the skills they need to be foster carers in the current fostering environment. Some fostering services have provided foster carers with mentors to support the development of these skills; others work with small groups of foster carers. Whatever means is provided, or suggested, to enable foster carers to reach an expected level of written and spoken English to fulfil their foster carer responsibilities, the fostering service and their SSW have to consider for each foster carer their learning style, to make sure that the chosen option will be effective, whether it be attending a local further education college or adult education course, group work provided by the fostering service or one-to-one support.

Identifying support, training and development opportunities that would benefit the quality of foster care offered by a foster carer is a skilled piece of work undertaken by the SSW and the foster carer. Foster carer development needs can be crudely categorised into five areas, although in reality they often overlap. The categories are: necessary development that becomes apparent through the work that a foster carer undertakes; generic areas applicable to all foster carers and foster children; those related to the specific circumstances of particular foster children; those related to the requirements of placements types; and lastly national and international training programmes devised to develop foster carers' knowledge and skills to facilitate foster children's development and management of their behaviour, such as Fostering Changes and KEEP. I will discuss each here in turn, but Fostering Changes and KEEP are discussed later in this chapter.

Necessary development that becomes apparent through the work that a foster carer undertakes

Devising and reviewing a foster carer's personal development plan, by the foster carer and their SSW, should take account of and build upon the foster care they have done in the previous year. This work enables the identification of areas of the foster carer's positive practice that can be built upon and developed, as well as noting areas of work with: their foster child; the foster child's family; school, health or other professionals responsible with the foster carer for the child's care plan, where they struggled or found it difficult. Difficulties are best addressed through supervision, in combination with training and development opportunities being made available to a foster carer, to make sure that the learning is integrated into the foster carer's practice, and their development built upon in supervision.

Generic areas applicable to all foster carers and foster children

Each foster child is different, and the supervision of their foster carer by the SSW has to be tailored to the particular foster care of a specific child. But when it comes to training, there are generic areas applicable to foster care that can be purposefully delivered to foster carers, irrespective of the particular child they care for. Such areas include for example: facilitating contact with a foster child's family; meeting the mental and physical health needs of children; enhancing educational outcomes for foster children (Berridge, 2012; Fursland, Cairns and Stanway, 2013); recording; being an effective member of the team around a foster child; legislation and policy relevant to foster care; court proceedings for children who are looked after; attachment, transition and loss; enabling a foster child to develop and build a positive sense of their history, identity, ethnicity and nationality; facilitating a child valuing and participating in their religion, where this is relevant; helping children recover from trauma; placement story work; assisting foster children to manage their behaviour; making possible foster children's participation in musical, artistic, dramatic, sport and social activity to enhance their resilience; managing health and safety matters at the same time as enabling sensible risk taking for children and young people; the impact of neglect, and sexual, physical and emotional abuse; and the foster carer's role in enhancing foster children's resilience. The list could go on and on, the point being that all the subject areas in the list above are relevant to all foster carers, irrespective of who they foster. For instance, attachment, transition and loss are subjects that foster carers need to understand to care for foster children, because all foster children experience attachment, transition and loss. The SSW, with the foster carer, will agree when, and how, the foster carer will learn about and consider the subjects above according to the stage of their foster care career, and congruent with the work they have done, and will be doing, caring for foster children.

Development related to the specific circumstances of particular foster children

In addition to generic areas of training, relevant to all foster carers and children, there are subjects specific to the care of particular foster children, and their individual care plans, about which a foster carer will need training and development opportunities to enable them to foster that child well. For instance, if a foster carer takes on a child with a chronic health condition, or a particular physical or learning disability, specific training and development opportunities may need to be identified for the foster carer to enable that child to be safe and well cared for, and the development of their own personality and abilities to be made possible. Such training might be facilitated by the fostering service, but sometimes can be delivered individually to a foster carer by hospital staff, or a community paediatric nurse, or an occupational therapist or psychologist, depending on the foster child's particular circumstances. The care of particular children requires a foster carer to deploy different knowledge and skills. Caring for a drug-dependent baby requires different knowledge, skills and attributes, as well as some that are the same, from caring for a drug- and alcohol-dependent 15-year-old young woman who is currently on a Youth Referral Order, with a related curfew, and a fitted electronic tag, placed with a foster carer on remand, awaiting trial for burglary.

Additionally areas of training and development identified in a foster carer's PDP can arise from the nature of a foster child's development during their placement. For example, if a young person comes out while placed with a foster carer as gay, lesbian or transgender, this might not have been a situation that the foster carer had envisaged when their foster child was placed with them 11 years earlier, and they might feel deskilled and thrown. In such situations some foster carers need support and supervision to enable them to manage their own feelings, if they are negative, thus enabling them to support and help their young person develop a positive view of themselves, and confidently handle some of the difficulties that young lesbian, gay and transgender young people might experience (Brown, forthcoming).

Other areas in which foster carers who care for particular children might need support, training and development for them to foster effectively include, for example: children and young people with mental health problems; children and young people who self-harm; school exclusion; young people who are being exploited, sexually, financially or otherwise; and young people who go missing.

Training and development related to the requirements of placement types

Training and development planning for foster carers is sometimes necessary to enable the foster carer to meet the requirements of their role and responsibilities, because of the nature of the foster care placement being suggested. For example: parent and child placements; support foster care; short breaks foster care; moving children on to permanent placements, whether adoption or permanent foster care, special guardianship or a residence order or a return to live with their birth family; helping young people move on to living independently; caring for sibling groups; family and friends foster care; considering caring for a foster child as a permanent member of the fostering family.

A foster carer who has expressed an interest in caring for a separated, unaccompanied young person seeking asylum in the UK would benefit from support and training about how best they could care for that young person, and work with other professionals and organisations to enable that young person's safe and comfortable development. Wade *et al.*'s (2012) research study, looking at fostering separated, unaccompanied asylum-seeking young people, revealed that foster carers who themselves had experienced migration felt better prepared to care for young people who had themselves, by definition, experienced migration, than foster carers who had not migrated. However, for those foster carers who had not experienced migration preparation for caring for these young people enabled them to feel better able to foster them. Nonetheless, although training and preparation is important, it is often a one-off event, or is time limited over a number of weeks, and thus the impact can be short lived. To maintain the learning and development that a foster carer accrues through training, it needs to be built upon through ongoing SSW supervision, to enable the benefits to be sustained and built upon.

Foster carers doing it for themselves

For the most part foster carers are people with agency, who, as well as relying on their fostering service and SSW to provide development and training opportunities, can develop their skills and ideas regarding fostering through their own volition by reading, attending seminars and conferences and accessing online resources about foster care, from such organisations as: the Fostering Network; the British Association for Adoption and Fostering; and the Social Care Institute for Excellence. The Department of Education in 2012, with the British Association for Adoption and Fostering, the Fostering Network, the Nationwide Association of Fostering Providers, and the Who Cares? Trust, developed an online group, the Fostering Information Exchange, to share practice, ideas and information about resources (Department of Education, 2013d). This forum provides an excellent opportunity for foster carers to engage with discussions regarding foster care.

Accessing online resources and reading relevant books and papers about foster care can be noted by the SSW as part of a foster carer's PDP. General texts about fostering (Schofield and Beek, 2006; Schofield and Simmonds, 2009: Fahlberg, 2008; Wheal and Mehmet, 2012) are useful for foster carers to read and then discuss with their SSW. Looking together in supervision at how the information is gleaned, and the ideas are stimulated, connects to their foster care and their care of specific foster children. All these texts are informative and accessible. Both the Fostering Network and the British Association for Adoption and Fostering have resources for foster carers and about foster care that can be accessed and utilised as part of a foster carer's PDP.

CASE STUDY 6.1

Daniel is a single carer, who works part time as a primary school teacher. He and his partner Abdul live separately, but Abdul stays at Daniel's house usually two nights a week. Daniel has been a foster carer for two years, and cared for twin nine-year-old boys for 18 months, who eventually moved on to live with their adult sister.

Daniel is currently caring for Sean, a mixed heritage, Irish and Pakistani, 16-year-old young person. Sean jokes about Daniel and Abdul exactly reflecting his heritage; Daniel being Irish, and Abdul Pakistani. This is Sean's 12th placement; he has been in care since he was three. Sean is subject to a Care Order and a Youth Referral Order, is fitted with an electronic tag and has to observe a curfew as part of his Youth Referral Order. He has been placed with Daniel for five weeks, during which time he has not had a school placement, but has reduced his cannabis use dramatically.

Daniel, Poppy (Daniel's SSW) and Craig (Sean's social worker) think the placement, to date, is going well. Craig is negotiating with the local authority to secure an educational placement in a local Pupil Referral Unit. Sean has not attended school in four years.

Daniel and Poppy are reviewing Daniel's PDP, in preparation for his annual foster carer review. They consider this work using the above framework:

1. **Necessary development that became apparent through the work that a foster carer did in the previous year.** *Poppy has become aware that Daniel, being assertive, and as a teacher knowing a lot about education, has 'put the backs up' of various professionals he has worked with, since Sean has been placed with him. Daniel is furious that Sean has been allowed to drift without a school place for so long; it seems inconceivable to him that Sean's Corporate Parent would have allowed this to happen. Poppy has had to manage Daniel's perceived aggressive phone conversations with an educational psychologist, and with Sean's social worker. To be an effective foster carer and advocate for Sean, Daniel needs to be able to work assertively, but effectively, with others responsible for Sean. Daniel agrees that 'losing his rag' is not effective; it is something he would never do as a teacher. Poppy and Sean agree that they will identify 'working effectively as part of the team around the child' in their supervision sessions as an ongoing agenda item. Poppy will see if there are any training opportunities coming up regarding this as well, for social workers and foster carers in the fostering service.*

2. **Generic areas applicable to all foster carers and foster children.** *Daniel has been waiting to go on a course, which has now become available, on attachment, transition and loss. Poppy and Daniel agree that he will attend this two-day event in a nearby city, run by another fostering service.*

3. **Those related to the specific circumstances of particular foster children.** *Daniel has been successful in helping Sean reduce his cannabis use, but does not know how this has happened, other than by talking with Sean, but he suspects this might be part of the 'honeymoon' period of the placement, and Sean's cannabis use might revert, over*

(Continued)

95

time, to what it was when he was first placed with Daniel. Poppy and he agree that they will both look for materials regarding drug use and young people, to read and use in their supervision sessions. Poppy will also look at what courses are available in the next six months about working with young people who use drugs.

4. **Those related to the requirements of placements types**. *Daniel thinks he needs support to develop his skills to help prepare Sean for moving on to independent living when he is ready. This is his first placement of a young person. He is aware he does a lot for Sean, because it is easier than getting him to do things himself, like putting on a wash, or cooking an occasional meal. Sean is aware that caring for young people requires him to develop the ability to help young people gain skills, such as budgeting, planning, cooking, cleaning, finding educational opportunities, work, etc., rather than continuing to act for them, and as a result, unwittingly decreasing their potential abilities. Poppy and Daniel agree that they will work together on this in supervision, and that Daniel will attend the fostering service's course on 'caring for adolescence and transitions to adulthood'.*

5. **National and international training programmes devised to develop foster carers' knowledge and skills to facilitate foster children's development and management of their behaviour such as Fostering Changes and KEEP**. *As with all of Poppy's fostering service's foster carers, Poppy and Daniel agreed some time ago that Daniel would attend the agency's Fostering Changes course, once his TSDS portfolio was successfully completed. The course is running in February and Daniel is looking forward to it.*

The Training Support and Development Standards (TSDS)

In 2007 the then Children's Workforce Development Council (CWDC) developed the Training, Support and Development Standards for foster carers. The Department for Children, Schools and Families and the CWDC's intention, at the time, was to ensure that *the Standards will play a key role in ensuring that providers make available to their carers appropriate opportunities for development, and that they support them in developing the skills and competence covered by the framework* (Department for Education and Skills, 2007, pp50–1). The current Department of Education's suite of Guidance regarding the Training, Support and Development Standards for foster carers makes clear that foster carers have to provide evidence to their fostering service, in the form of a workbook, that they have achieved the Standards within the first year after their approval. There are seven Standards as follows:

Understanding the principles and values essential for fostering children and young people; understand your role as a foster carer; understand health and safety and healthy care; know how to communicate effectively; understand the development of children and young people; safeguard children and young people and develop yourself.

(Department of Education, 2012b, pp11–52)

The Department of Education published further Guidance in 2012 about the TSDS for 'general' foster carers (TSDS) (Department of Education, 2012b), for family and friends foster carers (Department of Education, 2012c), short breaks foster carers (Department of Education, 2012d) and for support foster carers (Department of Education, 2012e).

A number of fostering services use the TSDS in creative and facilitative ways, helping foster carers reflect on the detail of their fostering practice with a specific child. However, an evaluation of its effectiveness in fulfilling the original Department for Children, Schools and Families' and the CWDC's aims will be important to assess whether it has been an effective intervention for both foster carers and, most importantly, foster children.

Unfortunately the TSDS workbook that foster carers have to complete is worded in such a way that suggests that through its successful completion foster carers will have met the Standards, rather than it being used for the development of foster carers through an ongoing process as was its original intention. The completed workbook has to be signed off by a foster carer's fostering service. The wording of the 'sign off' section is as follows: *I certify that the above named foster carer has successfully met all the outcomes in the Training, Support and Development Standards for Foster Care* (Department of Education, 2012f, p29). This sentence seems to imply that the completion of the booklet and the meeting of the Standards is one and the same thing, and that it is a time-limited exercise, rather than an ongoing developmental process.

There is an underlying assumption in the Department of Education's commitment to training and support for foster carers that it is effective. Therefore it will be important that the current TSDS workbook completion is evaluated regarding its impact on the quality of foster care, as at the present time it is consuming considerable resources of foster carers, SSWs and fostering services. The Government's emphasis on the importance of training for foster carers is based, presumably, on the assumption that training is effective in improving the quality of foster care. However, is this assumption grounded in evidence?

What the research tells us about the effectiveness of training for foster carers

Mehmet writes, *training is a central and intrinsic part of fostering and all agencies must have a clear plan for the training and development of all who work in the service* (Mehmet, 2005, p34). However, training offered to foster carers has varied in quality, content, structure and theoretical coherence. This lack of consistency in the quality of ongoing post-approval training, offered to foster carers, was recognised in the Government White Paper Care Matters: *In order for carers to provide the supportive commitment which is essential for children's development, they themselves must be provided with effective training and support* (Department for Education and Skills, 2007, p50).

Regarding the question of whether or not training for foster carers is effective in improving the quality of foster care, the 'jury remains out'. What is clear from the research evidence is that specific training that has a theoretical base, is well structured and coherent, builds on foster carers' experience and is linked to particular interventions seems to be more effective than 'general', one-off training events (Pallett, Blackeby, Yule, Weissman and Scott, 2005). The problem is that most foster carers receive 'general' training, on particular topics, rather than a coherent training programme, although this is changing with the rolling out of the Fostering Changes and KEEP training programmes. The one coherent training programme that all foster carers are likely to undertake is that which is delivered at the time of their assessment as prospective foster carers, prior to their approval; the Skills to Foster preparation training programme (The Fostering Network, 2009).

The Social Care Institute for Excellence's review of the research literature on foster care (Wilson *et al.*, 2004) and Pithouse, Young and Butler (2002) found little evidence that training of foster carers improved the quality of foster care. There are a number of studies that suggest that foster carers value training (Minnis, Devine and Pelosi, 1999; Triseliotis, Borland and Hill, 2000; Minnis, Pelosi, Knapp and Dunn, 2001; Ogilvie, Kirton and Beecham, 2006). However, valuing and enjoying training does not necessarily correlate with improving the quality of care of, and effective intervention with, foster children. In the Ogilvie *et al.* study (2006), 68 per cent of the foster carers who attended training rated it as very good or good. However, in the Triseliotis *et al.* study (2000) about the delivery of foster care in 32 Scottish authorities, they found that both carers and managers perceived there to be a lack of coherence in the training that foster carers received. *Like many carers, managers referred to continued training being 'periodic'; as having 'no cohesion'; 'erratic'; 'no pattern'; 'variable' or 'irregular'* (2000, p73). Sellick *et al.*, reviewing the research on the effectiveness of training for foster carers, conclude: *There are few studies of effectiveness of training carers. Research is needed which differentiates between types of training and evaluates content, process and outcomes of the programmes* (2004, p56). Wilson *et al.* confirmed this position, arguing that there is a *lack of evidence that specific forms of training can, on their own, improve outcomes* (2004, p67). Talbot and Wheal (2005) also argue that there has been little research into the effectiveness of training or its evaluation.

The critical litmus test for evaluating the effectiveness of foster carer training has to be whether or not it impacts beneficially on foster children. One study, using a randomised control trial, conducted in Scotland, concluded that training had been well received by foster carers, but it did not have a significant impact on the emotional well-being of the foster children (Minnis *et al.*, 2001). However, Ogilvie *et al.* (2006) cite a number of studies that indicate that training has been shown to have a beneficial effect in relation to: lower rates of placement breakdown; more openness to working with birth families and positive impacts on retention of foster carers. However, they also note that evaluations that look at the impact of training for foster carers have shown limited effects on children and carers . . . *thus the case for seeing training as a means of improving child outcomes remains unproven* (2006, p14). It would seem then that the assumption that training, per se, is a good thing has little or no evidence base. The current position is best summed up by Sinclair when he writes, *in general the studies provide plenty of evidence that carers appreciate training . . . Despite this praise the studies provided little evidence that current training has much effect on outcomes* (2005, p119).

SSWs, in line with the expectations set down by the NMS (Department of Education, 2011b), place considerable importance on working with foster carers to encourage them to attend training. Training expectations are set out in foster carers' PDPs and annual review paperwork. Occasionally difficulties that are encountered in a foster carer's practice, by their fostering service, are not worked with directly by their SSW, but rather the foster carer is encouraged to attend related training; for example, to develop skills in managing difficult behaviour, as if that in itself would improve the quality of their work. The evidence from the research above calls such social work practice into question.

However, there are positive evaluations of training programmes foster carers undertake, and the impact that training can have on their care of foster children, and on the foster children themselves. These positive examples are linked to specific training programmes, and specific foster care initiatives, rather than to foster carer training more generally. Two such current examples in the UK are Multidimensional Treatment Foster Care (MTFC) and the related KEEP training programme, and the Fostering Changes training programme. An understanding of foster care, as an intervention, was recognised by the Government by its funding of both the MTFC pilots, and the rolling out of the Fostering Changes training programme, both of which are designed to facilitate foster carers' purposeful and effective interventions in children's lives.

Fostering Changes

Fostering Changes is a UK-developed foster carer training programme that was set up in 1999 by the National Specialist Adoption and Fostering Team at the Maudsley Hospital, with King's College in London. The programme focuses on behaviour management, and the formation of positive and productive relationships between foster carers and their foster children. Pallett, Scott, Blackeby, Yule and Weissman (2002) and Warman, Pallett and Scott (2006) summarise the original programme's content, structure, process and effectiveness. More recently the programme has been revised to take account of the educational needs of foster children as well as placing emphasis on communication (Bachmann, Blackeby, Bengo, Slack, Woolgar, Lawson and Scott, 2011).

The theoretical underpinning of this 12-week programme is social learning theory and attachment theory. The programme has a clear structure (Briskman, Castle, Blackeby, Bengo, Slack, Stebbens, Leaver and Scott, 2012, pp12–18), and underlying values and principles that the programme team believes enhances the learning of participants. For example, importance is placed on valuing foster carers and their experience. Recognising that foster carers attendance at training can sometimes be a problem, the training team visits foster carers at home before the programme starts. The purpose of this is to engage foster carers, and gather information about their experience, and the practicalities of attending training at the same time as meeting the requirements of their role as a foster carer for specific children. The rate of retention of foster carers throughout the Fostering Changes programme is high (Pallett *et al*., 2002; Briskman *et al*., 2012). The ethos of the programme includes the conviction that the foster carers should have fun while attending.

Pallett *et al.*'s 2002 evaluation of the programme *suggests this training brings about improvements in the emotions and behaviour of the children in their care, and a better quality of relationship and interactions with them. It also has a beneficial effect on carers' sense of confidence and self-efficacy* (2002, p47). Warman *et al.*'s 2006 paper confirmed continuing effectiveness and acknowledged that it might be the approach of the programme, as much as the content, that contributed to its success. The approach is one of active learning and collaborative participation with peers. *Learning in this context is a process in which participants are encouraged to play an active role, both inside and outside the 'classroom'* (Warman *et al.*, 2006, p27). The strengths of the Fostering Changes programme are linked to its collaborative model of learning, which is underpinned by a specific theoretical base. Because the programme runs for 12 weeks it gives participants the opportunity to learn over time, within a safe and comfortable learning environment. These features might be important contributory factors, alongside the content of what is delivered contributing to Fostering Changes' success, in improving outcomes for both foster carers and their foster children.

Having developed a training manual for this programme, the Maudsley team was keen, as was the Government (Department for Education and Skills, 2007), that the Fostering Changes programme was evaluated, and this seemingly effective training programme rolled out to more local authorities and independent fostering services. In 2012 the Department of Education published the findings of a randomised control trial evaluating the effectiveness of the Fostering Changes training programme. Like the previous evaluations, noted above, the findings showed positive impacts of the programme on foster carers' care of children, and the children they cared for, in regards to the behaviour of foster children, and attachment security. Importantly the foster carers felt more confident as foster carers to be able to effect positive change.

> *Results from this trial demonstrate that this training provides the knowledge and practical skills that enable carers to enhance child behaviour and security. This should improve longer-term outcomes for looked after children and increase placement stability. The findings support Department of Education's decision to roll-out the programme nationally, and provide evidence for its continued use.*
>
> (Briskman *et al.*, 2012, p3)

There are particular aspects of the Fostering Changes programme that can be incorporated into the practice of SSWs and social workers responsible for a foster child. One of the strengths of the programme is that the foster carer is required to keep a diary about their own and their foster child's behaviour, and their relationship with their foster child, so that they can consider, with guidance, what they have done well, and what they might need to change.

> *. . . the Fostering Changes model does focus on the foster carers' relationship with the children they look after as the medium for bringing about change. The ways that carers relate to children in their care are recognised as having immense significance. How they talk to children, the language they use, their ability to listen, the ways that they respond to appropriate as well as inappropriate behaviour, are all seen to affect the child and the tenor of the relationship.*

This training therefore encourages carers to act 'differently' and enables them to provide new and subtly different experiences for the children in their care, which can improve how children think and feel about themselves, their immediate relationships and the world around them.

(Warman *et al.*, 2006, p20)

It seems that there are many benefits to foster carers, and their foster children, of being part of the Fostering Changes training programme, not only because of the expertise of those running the sessions, and the content, but also from the experience of learning from peer foster carers.

Multidimensional Treatment Foster Care (MTFC)/ Keeping Foster Parents Trained and Supported, KEEP

MTFC

MTFC and KEEP, like Fostering Changes, are evidence-based programmes. MTFC was developed and positively evaluated at the Oregon Social Learning Centre in the United States of America (USA). Roberts, Scott and Jones (2005), Biehal, Dixon, Parry and Sinclair (University of York) and Green, Roberts, Kay, Rothwell, Kapadia and Roby (University of Manchester) (2012) offer descriptions of the programme and how it is being implemented in the UK. The Government-funded MTFC pilot projects in England, as part of their Care Matters' (Department for Education and Skills, 2007) commitment to improving the quality of foster care, and from 2011 MTFC, and the related foster carer training programme KEEP, became part of the Department of Education's interventions for children looked after (National Implementation Team, 2011).

The MTFC programme is based on social learning theory and aims to improve outcomes for troubled children in public care who might otherwise be in custody or residential provision or do poorly in foster care. Each child and foster family has a trained, multi-professional clinical team working with them involving health, education and social services. MTFC covers a range of children and is divided into age-specific programmes: MTFC-P, for 3 to 6 year olds; MTFC-C, for 7 to 11 year olds; and MTFC-A, for 11 to 16 year olds. The MTFC programme content is prescribed, and fidelity to the model is considered important as a factor contributing to success. *Evidence from a number of trials concludes that treatment fidelity is a major determinant of outcome and that a high level of fidelity and model adherence is associated with positive outcomes* (National Implementation Team, 2008, p5).

Training of the foster carers involved in the projects is an important aspect of the successful outcomes for the foster children involved. Foster carers recruited to be part of the MTFC projects are assessed and approved by their fostering service, and undertake the Skills to Foster training programme, the same as other foster carers in the UK. These foster carers then undertake additional training about the MTFC model.

They then receive the additional training in the relevant MTFC model. This provides the basic information needed to understand the principles and practice of operating the programme in the foster carers' home. The two-day training course includes a number of case examples, practice exercises and role-plays,

Briskman, J, Castle, J, Blackeby, K, Bengo, C, Slack, K, Stebbens, C, Leaver, W and Scott, S (2012) *Randomised Controlled Trial of the Fostering Changes Programme*. London: National Academy for Parenting Research, King's College London/London: Department of Education.

This provides a comprehensive overview of the Fostering Changes programme as well as its evaluation.

Price, JP, Chamberlain, P, Landsverk, J and Reid, J (2009) KEEP Foster-parent Training Intervention: Model Description and Effectiveness. *Child and Family Social Work*, 14: 233–42

The paper gives an overview of KEEP and its effectiveness.

Chapter 7
Foster carer reviews

CHAPTER OBJECTIVES

By the end of this chapter, readers should:

- be familiar with the regulatory and good practice guidance regarding foster carer reviews;
- understand what is required to ensure that foster carer reviews are effective mechanisms for ensuring the quality of foster care for individual children, and foster care in general;
- appreciate how our own social work practice, in respect of foster carer reviews, can be further enhanced.

Introduction

A key mechanism for improving the quality of foster care is through foster carer reviews. They are conducted in order to evaluate a foster carer's practice, and offer the opportunity for improving the quality of foster care (Brown, 2011). Foster carer reviews provide a formal arena to consider: the quality of each foster carer's care of individual foster children; how the foster carer's development can be enhanced to enable them to improve their practice; and how a fostering service can support them to undertake their complex work. Reviews act as a vehicle for improving individual foster carer's support, supervision and practice.

There is surprisingly little published about foster carer reviews other than that which is within Regulation, Standards, Guidance and Codes of Practice. Indeed reviews of research about foster care are notably quiet on the subject (Berridge, 1997; Schofield, 2003; Sellick et al., 2004; Wilson et al., 2004; Sinclair, 2005; Sellick, 2006; Boddy, 2013). Reviewing foster carers is an area of social work and foster care practice that has attracted little research interest, despite reviews being a pivotal mechanism for the quality assurance of foster care. Mehmet (2005), Lawson (2011b) and Brown (2011) are three of the few people who have written about foster carer reviews. Mehmet, in her book about the UK National Standards for Foster Care (UKNSFC) (UK Joint Working Party on Foster Care, 1999a), the related Code of Practice (UK Joint Working Party on Foster Care, 1999b) and the then Fostering Services National Minimum Standards (Department of Health, 2002) (Mehmet, 2005), draws on the UKNSFC's detailed consideration of reviews. The UKNSFC, which have weathered the sands of time, and although dated and not legally binding, still have helpful things to say about good practice for foster carer reviews.

Writing about reviews in children and families work, but not specifically about fostering, Parker and Bradley write:

> *Review is seen . . . as a continuous process that considers what has been achieved from the planning stage and revises or refines accordingly, similar to an action-planning or action-research cycle. This requires social workers to develop a number of skills: planning; negotiating and consultation; information gathering; discussion and analysis; replanning.*

> (Parker and Bradley, 2010, pp123–4)

The relationship between the foster carer's original assessment and their reviews is fundamental. *Assessment is a process that continues throughout a foster carer's career and the first review in particular should build on the recommendations of the original assessment report* (The Fostering Network, 2010b, p59). Assessment, as noted in Chapter 4, offers the assessor's prognosis about a prospective foster carer's potential, whereas the review is where the detail of lived fostering experience can be evaluated. The positive circumstances, attributes, qualities and values of a foster carer, needed for them to become a foster carer, have to continue to be evidenced in reviews, through the detail of what the foster carer has actually done. Getting to this material in a review is unlikely to be realised through just asking direct questions, but rather will materialise through the carer telling the story of their fostering experience with specific foster children.

This chapter covers

- What the Standards, Guidance and Regulations say

- The review administrative process

- The SSW's report

- Facilitating contributors' input to foster carer reviews

- The review meeting.

What the Standards, Guidance and Regulations say

The Regulations and Guidance governing foster carer reviews are set out in:

- The Fostering Services (England) Regulations (Department of Education, 2011b, Regulation 28)

- The NMS (Department of Education, 2011a, Standards 13.8, 13.9 and 20.6)

- The Children Act 1989 Fostering Service Guidance (HM Government, 2011)

- The 2013 amendments to the Guidance and Regulations (Department of Education, 2013b, p18).

Reviews have to happen annually, and the first review within a year of a foster carer being approved. The foster carer review's regulatory function is to consider: whether or not the foster carer continues to be suitable to be a foster carer; that their household continues to be a suitable environment for fostering; and that their terms of approval remain appropriate (Department of Education, 2011b, p17, Regulation 28 (4) a and b). For those judgements to be made the Regulations require that views are sought from all social workers who have been responsible for any foster children placed with the foster carer, in the year since the foster carer's last review; or in the case of a newly approved foster carer in the year since their approval. The views of foster children, placed with the foster carer, must be sought, as well as the views of the foster carer themselves. In addition to the bare regulatory minimum, best practice requires that the views of the foster carer's own children, anyone else living in the household and third parties are also gathered. Third parties include those involved with the foster carer and the foster child, for example: schools; health visitors; nurseries; CAMHS; or the Youth Offending Service. Gathering these views provides triangulated evidence about the quality of foster care that the foster carer is affording children.

The administrative process

Effective administration of foster carers' reviews is key to them being undertaken in a timely, rigorous and inclusive manner. *There must be robust administrative and quality assurance arrangements for ensuring reviews take place on time and are undertaken appropriately to the circumstances of foster carers and the children placed* (Parrott et al., 2007, p141).

In Chapter 3 it was noted that a number of inquiry reports highlighted that foster carer reviews had not been conducted within the required regulatory timeframes: *Although fostering reviews took place, they did not happen annually, as required by Regulations, and it is not clear what information was presented to the Fostering Panel following each review* (Rotherham Safeguarding Children Board, 2010, p3). In the usual course of events reviews take place annually, but a fostering service can conduct a review at any time they see fit, and at whatever frequency as long as the minimum regulatory requirements are met (Department of Education, 2011b).

Conducting a foster carer's first review within six months, rather than within a year as required by regulation, after a first placement is made, or within the year, whichever is the sooner, is helpful. As noted in Chapter 3 the Wakefield Inquiry team recommended that newly approved foster carers should be reviewed *much earlier than the current statutory requirement* (Parrott et al., 2007, p141).

As discussed above it is best that the RO for a foster carer's review is not the SSW's line manager, thus enabling some degree of independent appraisal. The UKNSFC advised that the *review meeting is chaired by an appropriate third party, who can form an independent judgement and is knowledgeable about foster care* (UK Joint Working Party on Foster

Care, 1999a, p46). Many fostering services use ROs who are independent of the fostering service, thus enabling a greater degree of independence.

Reviews can be triggered by an allegation that has been made about a foster carer, or where there has been a change of circumstances for the foster carer and/or their household. The investigation of an allegation should be conducted separately from the review, and as discussed in Chapter 5 there has to be a clear distinction drawn between an investigation into an allegation and an exploration of a standard of care concern. It is most productive to conduct the review once the investigations have been completed. However, this is subject to the regulatory timeframes being met.

The quality of the paperwork gathered prior to a foster carer's review meeting is crucial as the RO is dependent on this documentation to inform their preparation for chairing the review meeting. The completion of reports for a foster carer's review should enable the engagement of the various individuals who can inform the review process. For foster carers and SSWs the writing of their reports enables informed reflection upon, and evaluation of, the quality of the foster carer's practice.

Fostering services vary in how they structure the different contributors' reports for foster carer reviews. This variation can be a strength but we need to make sure that all reviews incorporate areas that should be included. At the time of writing BAAF was piloting new foster carer review paperwork (BAAF, 2013b).

The SSW report

The SSW's evaluative report for the review, however structured, needs to address the foster carer's capacity to facilitate a foster child's safe, healthy, educational and emotional development; and to provide evidence that the foster carer is meeting the NMS (Department of Education, 2011a) requirements and the TSDS (Department of Education, 2012b). The report provides the opportunity for a holistic appraisal of a foster carer's work. The SSW analyses and synthesises the material they present in their report to enable evidence-based judgements to be made about: the quality of the foster carer's work; whether or not they and their household continue to be suitable to foster; and if so whether or not their current terms of approval are still appropriate.

However sophisticated the format of the SSW's report, its usefulness will be dependent on the SSW's ability to evidence their report, and analyse the material they draw on in such a way that identifies strengths, areas for further development, patterns and concerns. This will enable sound judgements to be made about the quality of the fostering undertaken in the review period. SSW's reports have to be fluent, detailed and logical, and there must be evidence of reasoned analysis leading to a recommendation. Evidenced decision making, and the ability to differentiate fact from opinion, should be apparent. The Wakefield Inquiry identified failings in one of the SSW's reports presented for the foster carers' first review, in that it lacked sufficient analysis, and failed to identify worrying emerging patterns (Parrott *et al.*, 2007). To enable the identification of both worrying and positive patterns, the SSW has to be familiar with the content of the foster carer's original assessment report, and their subsequent review reports.

The SSW's report, whatever the format used, in addition to the above will need to cover the following.

Current circumstances

SSW reports have to cover the foster carer's current circumstances. If there have been any significant changes to the foster carer's own circumstances or to those of members of their household, or to the household's composition during the review period, these need to be noted and most importantly the implications for fostering explored.

The fostering story

This includes the placement story for each foster child placed with the foster carer during the review period. The SSW's report should provide chronologically the narrative of each placement. This enables all the parties, including the RO, to gain a holistic understanding of the foster carer's work.

The fostering household and its dynamics

The quality of the relationships within the fostering household, and what the impact of these relationships has been on foster children, should be considered in the SSW's report. This includes addressing the quality of the relationship of a fostering couple (where there is a couple fostering), the foster carer's relationship with their own children (where there are foster carer's own children) and the relationships between their own children and the foster child. The SSW should describe the lifestyle of the fostering household. For example, what sort of activities do they do with the foster child, what is the structure of an average weekday and weekend? When there is a couple fostering the report needs to address both of their fostering roles and responsibilities, and the quality of their individual foster care, as well as how they foster as a couple.

The SSW should describe the foster carer's home and state whether or not, in their professional judgement, it is a suitable environment for a foster child. They need to consider what the home feels like from the perspective of a foster child: is it warm and welcoming? This will require the SSW to be familiar with the whole house and garden (where there is one) and importantly the foster child's bedroom (Ferguson, 2010). This professional judgement about the home as a suitable environment for a foster child is in addition to the health and safety checks, and the safer care policies for the foster children. It is more about such things as: the care taken of a foster child's bedroom; how individualised is it; what toys and/or equipment does the foster child have; where does a foster child do their homework; where can a 17-year-old fostered young person study quietly when revising for their philosophy A-level exam?

The impact of fostering on the foster carer and their family

The SSW's report must include an appraisal of how a foster carer's family, and members of their household, experience fostering. This assessment will be informed by the work that the SSW has done with the foster carer's family, and from reports family members will have individually completed for the purposes of the review.

Highlights of the review period

Foster carer reviews are primarily about the fostering service making sure that a foster carer is still appropriate as such, and that the care they provide foster children is of a good standard. Reviews also offer the opportunity to address with the foster carer what they have done particularly well. It is important that the SSW throughout the year gathers evidence of the foster carer's abilities, and achievements.

Complaints and/or allegations

SSW reports need to explicitly address any concerns about, or complaints, or allegations against a foster carer that have arisen during the review period. It is helpful to have a section of the SSW's report that directly requires the SSW to address this area, and records the outcomes of any investigations or complaints processes. Importantly issues or concerns raised in the previous review, as well as any matters raised by the fostering panel, where applicable, should also be addressed so that any emerging patterns can be identified.

The quality of the foster carer's relationship with, and direct care of, foster children

Reviews must directly address the most fundamentally important aspect of fostering, that being the quality of the direct care of foster children. This includes evidence that a foster carer ensures that a foster child is well clothed, eats healthy, fresh food, is up to date with their medicals, visits the optician and dentist, has an established routine, is encouraged educationally as well as with their hobbies and leisure pursuits, etc. The report will also evaluate how the foster carer is managing delegated authority.

The SSW must comment on a foster carer's ability to: show warmth and affection to a foster child; enjoy the company of children; play with a foster child at an age-appropriate level; talk to a child or young person; facilitate contact with a child's birth family; set appropriate boundaries for a foster child to enable them to feel, and be, safe and cared for; and facilitate changes in a foster child's behaviour where this is needed, using evidence-based approaches that are both kind and containing.

The SSW should comment on the foster carer's capacity to understand the impact of loss, transition and change on a foster child, and to empathetically engage with them. For example, this can be evidenced by how a foster carer helps a child manage their feelings and behaviour stimulated by contact with a member of their birth family, or how they helped them settle into their home the first night they arrived.

The foster carer's ability to respect and value the familial, racial, national, linguistic, cultural and religious heritage of a child should be commented on within the SSW's report. This 'comment' should be more than just providing evidence that the foster carer has provided appropriate physical care and food for a foster child, and facilitated them locating the nearest place of worship appropriate to their religion (where relevant). Rather the SSW's appraisal should be about how the foster carer conveyed their interest in, respect for and engagement with the foster child's family, their history, their language, their country of origin, their religion and their culture.

SSW's reports must include their direct observations of the quality of a foster carer's relationship with the foster child, drawing on their planned contact with the child and foster carer, and from their unannounced visits. For example, how did the foster carer comfort, play with, talk to a foster child and/or manage their behaviour on a particular occasion observed by the SSW? Unannounced visits provide a snapshot of a foster carer's home, their lifestyle and the day-to-day experience of living in that foster home for foster children. However, they do only provide a snapshot.

The foster carer's facilitation of contact

A foster carer will usually be involved with their foster child's contact with their birth family. Dependent on the nature of the care plan, for the foster child, this involvement will range from, for example, taking a child five times a week to a contact centre to facilitating contact between their foster child and their parent in the foster carer's home on Saturdays. The SSW needs to evidence and appraise how a foster carer has facilitated contact for their foster child.

The quality of the foster carer's relationship with the fostering service

The quality of the working relationship between the SSW, the foster carer and the fostering service was identified in the Wakefield Inquiry to be a significant factor that was insufficiently explored in the foster carers' review (Parrott et al., 2007). The quality of the working relationship is crucial for effective communication and for making sure that a foster child is kept safe, and at the centre of everyone's attention.

In addition, the SSW should evaluate the foster carer's ability to meet all the bureaucratic requirements of the fostering service. These will include keeping financial records of how money is spent on the care of a foster child, and the quality of a foster carer's recordings about the foster child. Importantly the SSW's report has to evaluate the foster carer's ability to use supervision effectively, and apply what they have learnt to the direct care of a foster child.

The foster carer's relationship with other professionals

Foster care is primarily about the direct care of foster children, enabling their development and helping them reach their potential. But being a capable foster carer also requires the ability to work with a range of other professionals involved with the foster child. The foster carer is a member of the professional team around the child, responsible for the realisation of a foster child's care plan. Their contribution to that team and their effectiveness playing their proactive part has to be appraised by their SSW, and themselves.

The effectiveness of the foster carer's support network

The SSW needs to evaluate the effectiveness of the foster carer's support network, and comment on how it has been utilised. If the support network's composition needs reviewing, that should be identified as a target for the SSW and the foster carer, and discussed at the review meeting.

The foster carer's personal development plan (PDP)

As discussed in Chapter 6, the SSW needs to comment on the foster carer's PDP including training and development opportunities they have taken part in, and how the related learning has been utilised by the foster carer in their direct care of foster children. The SSW's report should include a PDP for the following year, agreed with the foster carer, about the foster carer's continuing development, including what training they will attend.

Targets to be achieved before the next review

The SSW's report usefully includes targets for themselves, the fostering service and the foster carer for the forthcoming year, as well as information about how targets set from the foster carer's last review have been realised.

Recommendation

The SSW's report should logically progress towards a substantiated, evidenced, recommendation regarding a foster carer's suitability to continue to be approved as a foster carer, and whether or not their terms of approval should remain the same or change. If they are recommending that the foster carer's terms of approval should change they need to state their reasons for this recommendation, if the foster carer is in agreement, and any related support that might be needed to enable this change. If the SSW is not recommending the foster carer's continued approval they need to set out their reasons, and what work has been done to enable the foster carer to make the required changes; thus providing a balanced report which highlights strengths and concerns.

Facilitating contributors' input to foster carer reviews

The fostering Regulations set a minimum requirement about whose views should be sought to inform foster carer reviews. These include: the foster carer; any foster child placed with the foster carer; and the social workers responsible for all foster children that have been placed with the foster carer since their last review or since their approval. The Regulations also state the fostering service must *make such enquires and obtain such information as they consider necessary in order to review whether the foster parent continues to be suitable to be a foster parent and the foster parent's household continues to be suitable* (Department of Education, 2011b, Regulation 28 (3) (a)). To obtain such information might involve seeking a wider set of views than just those that are suggested above. The UKNSFC propose, in addition to the SSW's report, seeking:

> the written views of each social worker responsible for any child placed in the foster home since the last review, the views of children who are fostered and their parents where appropriate, and the views of the carer, her and his sons and daughters and any other household members.

(UK Joint Working Party on Foster Care, 1999a, p46)

In addition to this, Mehmet recommends that members of a foster carer's support network also make a contribution as well as *Anyone else who can provide evidence . . .*, *e.g. teachers of the children* (2005, p109), thus enabling third-party evidence to be gathered. To review and evaluate the quality of a foster carer's practice, their continuing suitability to be a foster carer and the appropriateness of their current terms of approval there needs to be triangulation of evidence.

Foster carers' contribution

The foster carer's report is self-evaluative, and therefore needs to describe and appraise the fostering they have undertaken since their last review or, for those that have been approved in the last year, since their approval. Some foster carers need support to complete their review paperwork and this should be provided where necessary, enabling their full participation in the review process. However, it is likely, as a result of foster carers' completion of the TSDS, that they will be more familiar with self-evaluation than some had been hitherto.

Foster carers' reports ought to identify what they consider they have done well, and where they feel they could improve. The reports usually also identify how they think their SSW, and their fostering service, could support them with their foster care and development, including the identification of relevant training.

The foster carer needs to consider the care of each foster child that they have cared for, and/or continue to care for, during the review period. If a fostering service requires foster carers to make reference to the NMS (Department of Education, 2011a) or to the TSDS (Department of Education, 2012b) then, in so doing, the narrative of the review period should not be lost.

Foster children's contribution

All foster children who are currently placed with a foster carer must be asked to make a contribution to the foster carer's review (Department of Education, 2011b). In addition, it is good practice to ask foster children who were placed with the foster carer during the review period but are no longer placed with them for their contribution. Fostering services have developed a range of child-friendly ways to elicit foster children's contributions. I use the term 'contribution' as this can be made in different ways, not just through written reports. Some fostering services have developed imaginative age-appropriate review forms for foster children, and foster carers' own children, to complete incorporating drawings, the use of symbols and space to make their own individual contribution.

Fostering services need to clarify who facilitates the foster child's contribution: the SSW, the foster child's social worker or another adult such as a teacher? The foster child needs to be familiar with whoever approaches them. It is not appropriate for the foster carer to do this work with a foster child. A foster child might not want to, or cannot, complete a form because of their age or their ability. In such cases the SSW, the foster child's own social worker or another adult such as a teacher would interview them, recording accurately their responses to questions, and any of the child's own comments.

A foster child or young person's contribution to a foster carer's review is key to the overall evaluation of the quality of foster care being provided. The foster child's experience of being cared for by the foster carer is fundamentally important. Without their contribution the review will only be partial. The foster child needs to understand why they are completing a review report form, or why they are being interviewed, and how what they say or write will be used. They need to be engaged in an age-appropriate manner. Communicating with children and the best ways of helping children express what they think and feel are central to SSWs' and children's social workers' practice (Luckock and Lefevre, 2008; Thomas, 2009; Lefevre, 2010). Although none of these texts specifically address foster children's contributions to foster carer reviews, they look at communicating with children from different standpoints and usefully consider communication with disabled children, young children, adolescents and different media for communication including writing, drawing, games, play and talking.

For some social workers communicating with children raises anxiety, because they feel they lack the necessary skills. Thomas helpfully reminds us that:

> *Communicating with children and young people is not necessarily so very different from communicating with adults. Wherever people are in need, the basic requirements are the same – warmth, empathy, trust, and sensitivity to the person's verbal and non-verbal language and style of communication.*

> (Thomas, 2009, p66)

A foster child's contribution usefully can focus on what their experience is/was of being cared for by the foster carer, for instance, such areas as: what it was like when they arrived at the foster carer's home; were they made welcome; what they think of their bedroom, their clothes, toys, equipment and the food they are given; what it is like living with the foster family; how the foster carer helps them keep in touch with their birth family (where appropriate); if they can talk to their foster carer about any worries they have, or when they feel unhappy; how the foster carer helps them with their school work; who they would talk to if they were unhappy about something in their foster home.

The foster child needs to be given the opportunity to say anything that they want to, and not be limited by the adult's use of direct questions, or the format of a review report form. If a foster child is interviewed this should take place somewhere where the foster child feels comfortable. Similarly if a foster child is completing a review report form, thought needs to be given to how they will receive the form, and how the purpose of its completion will be properly explained. Some foster children want to complete their forms alone, whereas others value their social worker or the SSW being with them so they can discuss what they are writing.

Thomas notes the importance of non-verbal communication when he writes: *children's non-verbal communication can be just as important and revealing as their words, and sometimes more so* (Thomas, 2009, p66). This non-verbal communication should be noted when a child is being interviewed, and its significance analysed.

The foster carer's own children's contribution

Lawson reminds us that *the sons and daughters of foster carers are key components of the success of a placement and contribute significantly to promoting positive outcomes for children in foster care* (2011b, p25). Foster carers' own children ought to be given the opportunity to contribute to foster carers' reviews. The same applies to these children as that noted above for foster children. They need to be asked to make their contribution about what their experience is living in a fostering family, through whatever medium is considered the most appropriate for them as individuals. The following are important to include: who they would talk to if they were unhappy about anything related to fostering or a foster child? What are the good things about being in a fostering family, and what are the negatives?

The impact of fostering on a foster carer's own children is an important consideration for a fostering service. There might be times where the needs of a foster carer's own child should be the main focus for the foster carer and, as a result, they need to take a break from fostering to focus on their child.

The foster children's social worker's contribution, for all foster children placed during the review period

Regulations require foster children's social workers to contribute to the foster carer's review (Department of Education, 2011b). Social workers' views are important to inform the review meeting about the quality of foster care that their foster child received, or is receiving. They will be able to comment on the foster carer's ability to: work with the foster child's birth family around contact; work with other professionals including education and health; and to provide good quality direct care to the foster child.

The foster child's social worker's contribution to a foster carer's review has been shown to be important in Chapter 3. Their views are sometimes different from the SSW's, and exploring differing viewpoints in the review meeting can be important for informing safe decision making. Foster children's social workers are often busy, and might not see the completion of a report for a foster carer's review as a priority. Where a report is not forthcoming this needs to be dealt with by the fostering service's senior managers because the foster child's social worker's input is required by Regulation.

The foster children's parent's contribution (where appropriate)

Contributions from a foster child's parent/s about what they think of the quality of care their child has received, or is receiving, where possible should be sought. Their views will improve the depth of evaluation about the quality of the foster care being provided. In the sub-title of this section I have written '(where appropriate)'. This is because there might be specific circumstances when seeking the contribution of a foster child's parent/s would not be in a foster child's interest. In the majority of cases parents do not make contributions to foster carer's reviews, because they are not asked. Where they are asked, and they make a contribution, it is often helpful to the review process. A parent might raise a pertinent matter of which no other contributor to the review process is aware. Gaining their views adds to a holistic evaluation of a foster carer's work and increases the possibility of triangulation of evidence, to inform professional judgements and decision making.

Some parents might not want to complete a written review report form, and should be offered the opportunity of being interviewed face to face, or on the phone, or submitting their contribution by e-mail (where applicable). Standard 16.2 of the UKNSFC noted that the written views of the parent of a foster child (where appropriate) should be sought for a foster carer's review (UK Joint Working Party on Foster Care, 1999a, p46). The Government has reiterated the importance of working in partnership with parents. Guidance states: *parents should be expected and enabled to retain their responsibilities and to remain as closely involved as is consistent with their child's welfare, even if that child cannot live at home either temporarily or permanently* (HM Government, 2010, p3). The Guidance goes on to state that in line with the intention of the Children Act 1989 *parents should be encouraged to exercise their responsibility for their child's welfare in a constructive way . . .* (HM Government, 2010, p3). In the spirit of this Guidance it is important to gain a foster child's parent's views about the quality of the foster care that their child receives, and for them to contribute their views regarding how delegated authority is being enacted.

Third parties' contribution

As noted earlier the Regulations state that a fostering service must *make such enquires and obtain such information as they consider necessary in order to review whether the foster parent continues to be suitable to be a foster parent and the foster parent's household continues to be suitable* (Department of Education, 2011b, p17). At least one third party report, commenting on the quality of foster care, can enhance the quality of the review process. For example, reports can be sought from the foster child's: school; nursery; college; Children's Guardian; health visitor; CAMH's psychologist; Youth Offending Service social worker – whoever can make a meaningful evaluative contribution. Where a foster carer has done a particular piece of work, such as introducing a foster child to their adoptive parent/s, a report from the adoptive parents is useful.

Where a foster carer's child has experienced difficulties, within the review period, then third party reports relating to the impact of those difficulties on the suitability of the fostering household to continue to care for foster children should be sought. For example, if a foster carer's adult son, who lives at home, has been arrested for carrying an offensive weapon.

The contribution third party reports make can be invaluable, and give a different perspective from those of the foster carer, the foster child, the SSW and the foster child's social worker. When the reports are finally collected and collated the review paperwork should be sent to the RO, so they can prepare for chairing the review meeting.

The review meeting

Foster carer reviews should have a review meeting conducted, which takes place in a foster carer's home, before the final review paperwork is submitted to the fostering service and/or the fostering panel. The review meeting itself is central to the review process. It is where matters arising from the review reports can be properly explored. The deliberations of the review meeting and the content of the review reports inform the RO's report and their recommendation regarding the foster carer's continuing approval as a foster carer, and their terms of approval.

The review meeting is usually chaired by someone other than the SSW or the SSW manager. The UKNSFC Standard 16.6 states: *A review meeting is held that includes the carer and the supervising social worker, and is chaired by an appropriate third party, who can form an independent judgement and is knowledgeable about foster care* (UK Joint Working Party on Foster Care, 1999a, p46). Lawson (2011b) reiterates the importance of a review meeting being held, chaired by someone who does not have a direct relationship with the foster carer or SSW when he writes: *It is good practice to hold a meeting with the foster carer to consider all this information, and for this to be chaired independently by someone who is not in any way responsible for the foster carer's supervision* (2011b, p129). Many fostering services use independent social workers as ROs to chair foster carer reviews. Others use senior members of the fostering service, who do not have line management responsibility for the foster carer, and others draw from their pool of independent reviewing officers (IRO) for children who are looked after. Where fostering services use IROs for the purposes of the foster carer RO role, they need to be mindful of the Wakefield Inquiry recommendation, that for the foster carer review, *the chair should not be the same person who chairs reviews on the children who have been placed with the carers* (Parrott et al., 2007, p141).

To maximise the possibility of an 'independent judgement' being reached, wherever possible an RO should ideally be drawn from outside the fostering service, as they are more likely to be able to maintain an independent stance. That is not to say that ROs drawn from the fostering service cannot form 'independent judgements'. The most important factor to consider when identifying an RO to chair a foster carer review meeting is the capability of that RO. The only publication that addresses this is the Wakefield Inquiry, and there only in as much as the inquiry team recounted the RO's deficits. The inquiry report noted the importance of an RO's ability in *facilitating, analysis and weighing up information before arriving at conclusions* (Parrott et al., 2007, p92).

The RO should have the skills and knowledge to: critically read the review paperwork sent to them prior to the review meeting taking place; identify salient areas that need to be discussed at the review meeting, and any matters that need to be explored with relevant parties beforehand; formulate an agenda covering pertinent areas for all foster carer review meetings, as well as particular matters related to the specific foster carer; chair the meeting in a facilitative, inclusive and rigorous manner; draw out key matters explored in the review meeting; and write a RO's report that is analytic, logical and makes a substantiated and properly evidenced recommendation, drawing on the deliberations of the review meeting, and the review paperwork.

Preparations for the review meeting

The RO should read the review paperwork critically and analytically, thus enabling the identification of key areas to be explored during, or prior to, the review meeting. In so doing it is important that they identify any missing reports, and seek clarification as to why they are missing if this explanation is not present in the SSW's report. The RO needs to: become familiar with the content of the review paperwork and each of its component parts; identify any contradictory comments; note gaps in what has been commented upon, for example, there might be no mention made of the foster carer's ability to facilitate a foster child's involvement in leisure activities, or the quality of their relationship with a foster child's birth family, or how they are gathering mementoes from the placement for their foster child; identify any emerging themes; make sure that all regulatory requirements have been met including all necessary checks being up to date, and that targets from the previous review or those set by the approval panel or the fostering panel that considered the foster carer's last review have been realised. They should identify good fostering practice, and any areas of concern.

On reading the review paperwork the RO might identify further work that needs to be undertaken prior to the review meeting, or that they need to seek clarification about a particular matter raised, or an opinion voiced. When the RO reads the review paperwork, and it becomes apparent that a matter needs to be addressed prior to the review meeting itself, they ought to discuss this with the SSW, and the SSW manager. For example, a radically different view reported by a foster child's social worker and the SSW about the quality of care provided to a foster child would need exploration prior to the review meeting. In such cases, as was recommended in the Wakefield Inquiry, the RO should ask that this be explored and clarified by the fostering service prior to the review meeting.

The meeting itself

The purpose of the review meeting is for the RO, the foster carer and the SSW to evaluate the foster care undertaken during the review period. The RO needs the requisite interpersonal and chairing skills to enable the foster carer to participate in the review in such a way that enables them to feel respected and valued. It is their review. Where there have been concerns raised about the quality of their fostering, the foster carer must have the opportunity to give their perspective, and feel that this has been explored and noted.

I have referred throughout to 'foster carer' in the singular, for ease of reading. However, there are single foster carers, and couples who foster. It is important, in the case of couples, that both are present at the review meeting that addresses the fostering that each partner undertakes, and explores their respective relationships with the foster child and the SSW, rather than the review only addressing the foster care of just one person in the couple.

The review meeting is held in the foster carer's home. At the beginning of the review meeting the RO should make sure that the foster carer understands the regulatory requirements for foster carer reviews, and that the RO makes a recommendation about the foster carer's continuing approval and their terms of approval, and that the recommendation goes to the fostering panel and/or the fostering service. The final decision is made by the ADM. If there are concerns raised in the review paperwork that might lead to a recommendation terminating a foster carer's approval, this needs to be made explicit to the foster carer, by the fostering service, prior to the review meeting.

The RO role requires good interpersonal and chairing skills, as well as the ability to think in a critical and reflective way, to enable an open, honest, rigorous and foster-child-focused discussion. The RO needs to be mindful of both the content and the process of the review meeting. It is often the case that in addition to chairing the review meeting, the RO makes notes about what is said. If this is done the RO needs to explain to the foster carer why they are taking notes, and how the notes will be used.

Whatever the preferred review meeting agenda, it is the RO's responsibility to make sure that all necessary areas are covered in the review meeting, and that the following areas are discussed and explored:

- The review period.

- Any changes to the foster carer's circumstances, or to the composition of their household.

- Significant events for the foster carer and their family.

- Each placement story for each of the foster children placed during the review period. As well as a holistic review this should include: the quality of the direct care of each of the foster children, including the foster carer's emotional and physical care of the foster child; how they have managed any problematic behaviour and facilitated the foster child's education, physical and mental health, and overall development.

- Where the foster carer has their own children, how those children are doing, and what the impact is on them of being part of a fostering family.

- The quality of the working relationship between the foster carer and the SSW, and the fostering service. The foster carer's views about the support and supervision they are getting and what additional support would help them meet the requirements of their role and responsibilities.

- The quality of the working relationships between the foster carer and other professionals involved with the foster children placed during the review period.

- The quality of the foster carer's involvement with a foster child's contact arrangements, and with their birth family. The foster carer's ability to help a child make sense of their circumstances, and their placement story.

- The use made, and effectiveness of, the foster carer's Disclosure and Barring Service (DBS) checked support network.

- The foster carer's management of delegated authority.

- The foster carer's ability to work in accordance with the foster child's care plan, and related placement plan, and personal education plan.

- The foster carer's PDP, including what training and education they have undertaken, and how their learning has been utilised with foster children placed with them during the review period.

- Any allegations or complaints investigation's outcomes, and their implications for the foster carer's continued approval.

- That all checks required by Regulations and medical checks are up to date, and that any identified required actions from the most recent annual health and safety check on the foster carer's home are being dealt with. The safer care policy for the foster family and/or specific foster children are up to date and effective.

- Targets from the foster carer's last review, and matters raised in fostering panel minutes.

- Targets to be set for the period before the next review.

- The RO's recommendation regarding the foster carer's continuing approval, and the terms of approval and the rationale for both.

- Summing up: identifying areas of strengths, concerns and areas for further development.

- The date of the next review.

During the review the RO has the opportunity to meet the foster carer and hear their perspective on the review period, and their evaluation of the quality of the work they have done, as well as hearing the SSW's views. The foster carer and the SSW might want to provide evidence at the review meeting of excellent or good fostering practice. For example, a foster carer might have facilitated a successful introduction of an 18-month-old child to their adoptive parents. As a result of the quality of this work the adopters might have written to the foster carers thanking them for their work, which, in the adopters' view, gave a solid start to their relationship with their adopted child. Showing this letter to the RO is helpful as it can be drawn on in the RO's report as evidence of an effective piece of work that the foster carer has undertaken.

Asking the foster carer to describe particular events, to aid the exploration of the quality of their practice can bring the story and detail of their fostering to life. For example, how did the foster carer manage the arrival of a particular foster child? How was that foster child welcomed? How does the foster carer think the foster child felt when they arrived, and by the time they went to bed? These discussions can flesh out a foster carer's ability to empathise with a foster child, and throw light on their understanding of the emotional impact of separation, loss and transition on a foster child, and how they enabled a child to feel safe enough, both physically and emotionally.

How foster carers manage and intervene with foster children's problematic behaviour is important to discuss in the review meeting, because foster carers can play a central role in enabling children to change their behavioural patterns for the better. Exploring the detail of what the foster carer did to handle such behaviour, and their understanding of the foster child's actions, and the effectiveness of their response is helpful. The content of the SSW's supervision should be discussed, to ascertain that the foster carer is getting support, supervision and advice based on research evidence about what works in helping children with their behaviour. For example, supervision drawing on approaches discussed in Chapter 6, underpinned by social learning theory and attachment theory, utilised in such training programmes as Fostering Changes (Pallett *et al.*, 2005; Warman *et al.*, 2006; Bachmann *et al.*, 2011) and KEEP (MTFCE, 2013).

Where foster children have moved on in a planned way the RO should explore if there are any unresolved areas for the foster carer. Where the foster carer was strongly attached to a foster child, the RO should ascertain if they got support that enabled a successful transition for the foster child, and a satisfactory ending for themselves. Where a foster carer has precipitated an unplanned ending to a foster child's placement, the circumstances from the perspective of the foster carer, the SSW, the foster child's social worker and the fostering service need to be discussed, and any implications for future placements considered. The review meeting offers the opportunity for differences of opinion to be aired and addressed.

In the review meeting the RO can help identify the foster carer's strengths and concerns and where further development is needed. The RO has the opportunity to listen to the foster carer's detailed description of their care of, and relationship with, the foster child. It is important that the RO, as well as listening to the content of what is being said, is also sensitive to affect, gaps and themes that emerge. For example, it might become apparent that the foster carer speaks with warmth about a particular foster child, but not with such affection when talking about that foster child's older sister who they also foster. If such material is evident in the review meeting it is the RO's responsibility to identify it, so that the quality of the foster carer's relationships with their foster children can be fully discussed. The RO must explore all areas identified in the paperwork that raised concern, lacked clarity or were contradictory.

The RO's observational skills need to be deployed during the review meeting. The RO has the opportunity to observe first-hand the quality of the relationship between the foster carer and the SSW, and where there is a foster child at home the quality of the relationship between the foster carer and the foster child. Where a fostering couple is being reviewed the RO can observe the quality of interaction between the couple, as they discuss the fostering they have undertaken. It is important that anything of note observed by the RO, positive or concerning, is raised during the review meeting so that it can be explored, and the implications for fostering scrutinised. In addition, the RO has the opportunity to note the quality of the foster carers' engagement with them as the RO, for example how they were welcomed into the foster carer's home. RO's observations are only ever snapshots, on a particular day, and should be thus contextualised within the review meeting discussions, and within the RO's related report.

The RO sees the foster home at the review meeting, and can form a view as to its appropriateness as an environment for foster children. They can note evidence of foster children's physical presence or the lack of it, the emotional warmth of the home, and how the foster carer and their family are including a foster child through such things as displayed photographs and artwork. It is not the role of the RO to conduct a health and safety audit during the foster carer review. However, if the poor state of the home, or the care of a foster child's bedroom, has been raised in the paperwork the RO should ask to see the whole house and the foster child's bedroom to inform their independent judgement. The RO should not rely on the assessment of the original assessor or previous ROs because circumstances change.

As well as making sure that the review meeting offers the opportunity for a holistic evaluation of the foster carer's work, any specific concerns have to be explicitly addressed during the meeting. The RO needs to make sure that anything that might later be written in their RO's report has been covered with the foster carer, and the SSW. At the end of the review meeting it is helpful for the RO to summarise the main areas that have been discussed, identifying the strengths and any concerns that have been raised. As well as reviewing the planned PDP in the meeting, targets should be set to ensure that any concerns are addressed, and areas of development identified. Targets should include actions for the fostering service, SSW and foster carer, identifying timeframes and responsible people.

If the RO, at the end of the review meeting, thinks that they will be recommending that the foster carer's approval be terminated, they can either tell the SSW and the foster carer at the end of the review meeting itself that they will be making such a recommendation, or say that they are considering this but need to deliberate further through the writing of their report. If they decide to do the latter, it is incumbent on the RO, in my view, to produce their report in a matter of days after the review meeting, so that the foster carer is not left in a state of anxiety. The Wakefield Inquiry (Parrott *et al.*, 2007) identified a problem with delays with RO's reports being completed in a timely manner after the review meeting had been undertaken. If an RO is going to make a recommendation that a foster carer's approval should be terminated, they need to explain the processes involved to the foster carer, and ask that the SSW and the fostering service offer further clarification, and identify any necessary support.

CASE STUDY 7.1

Becky and Stan, a white English couple in their fifties, have been fostering for 12 years. Stan is a full-time foster carer and Becky works part time as a hotel receptionist. They live in a village six miles from a city in the north-west of England. Their three adult children live nearby, all with their own families. In total, Stan and Becky have fostered 25 children and young people, between the ages of 2 days and 17 years. At their last foster carer review a recommendation was made by their SSW and the fostering panel, agreed by the fostering service ADM, that their terms of approval would be changed to enable them to, once trained, have a parent and child placement, if one became available; this was something they have wanted to do for some time. As well as undertaking related training, with their fostering service, they also spent several supervision sessions with their SSW discussing what would be required of them when a parent and child placement was made.

Six months ago a white, Welsh, young woman of 16 (Bronwyn), whose previous foster placement of ten years had broken down, partly as a result of the ongoing rivalry between herself and another child placed with the family, which led to Bronwyn threatening the other young person with a knife, came to live with them. Bronwyn was six months pregnant at the time when she was placed with Stan and Becky.

At the time of Stan and Becky's impending review meeting Bronwyn's baby Crystal was three months old, and was thriving in her mum's and Becky and Stan's care. Bronwyn was subject to a Care Order and Crystal to an Interim Care Order. The local authority had serious concerns about Bronwyn's ability to sustain her care of Crystal. Since she was placed with Becky and Stan she stayed out for two unplanned nights away from Crystal. On another occasion when she was meant to have gone to visit her dad, instead Bronwyn took Crystal to see her brother, a known sex offender who she had agreed with the local authority she would not visit with her daughter. Bronwyn and Crystal are undergoing an assessment regarding Bronwyn's parenting capacity, which will inform the ongoing court proceedings for Crystal.

Karen, Becky and Stan's SSW, made sure that all the paperwork for the review meeting was prepared and sent to the RO in preparation for the impending review meeting. Bronwyn's written evaluation of the foster care she is receiving, for the purposes of Becky and Stan's forthcoming review, is glowing. Her report is full of such phrases as 'they could not be doing better in every way'. Bronwyn's mum's report is similarly full of hyperbole, containing statements like 'fantastic people', 'brilliant foster home', 'the best foster carers ever'. Becky and Stan's self-evaluative report indicates that they are thoroughly enjoying caring for Bronwyn, and adore Crystal. In addition their report is very negative about Bronwyn's previous foster carers.

However, Bronwyn and Crystal's social workers' reports raise real concerns about Becky and Stan's, in their view, collusive relationship with Bronwyn and their seeming inability to focus on Crystal's long-term best interests. Karen's SSW report raises some concerns about Becky and Stan's recordings, in that they seem to skirt around the three concerning incidents; the two when Bronwyn stayed out and did not let anyone know where she was, and her worrying visit to her brother. Karen is also aware that some foster carers find the monitoring and 'surveillance' elements required when caring for a parent and child difficult because of their attachment to both Bronwyn and Crystal. Karen thinks that the review meeting is an opportunity to address some of her concerns with the RO, Becky and Stan, so that they can reiterate the need to keep the focus on Crystal, and her related care plan, at the same time as caring for Bronwyn.

The local authority is clear that if another incident occurs where Bronwyn places Crystal at potential risk, or she leaves Crystal with Becky and Stan when that has not been agreed, that Crystal will be removed from Bronwyn. Becky and Stan's paperwork makes it clear that they don't think that should happen. Bronwyn has made three 'mistakes' but in their view she is competently caring for Crystal, with their support.

Points for the RO to consider from the case scenario, in preparation for the review meeting

- In addition to making sure that all the agenda items listed earlier in the chapter for the review meeting are covered, the RO might want to additionally make sure the meeting addresses:

  o what Stan and Becky have done well, particularly as Crystal is described by everyone, including in the third party health visitor's report for the purposes of the foster carer review, as thriving, as well as explicitly addressing concerns;

  o Bronwyn and Crystal's placement plans, and care plans, and how Becky and Stan are contributing to their realisation;

  o the content and regularity of the SSW's supervision of the foster carers, to ascertain what support and direction they are getting in making sure that their focus is on Crystal, at the same time as ensuring Bronwyn is held in mind.

- o the incongruent content of the various reports, and to elicit people's understandings of what that signifies;

- o the quality of the working relationships between Becky and Stan, and Crystal and Bronwyn's social workers, and Becky and Stan's SSW; to make sure that they are all working in line with Bronwyn and Crystal's care plans, and that Becky and Stan are effective members of the teams around Bronwyn and Crystal;

- o any other areas you would want to make sure were discussed. Remember this is the foster carer's review, not Bronwyn's or Crystal's review.

The RO could direct the SSW to useful parent and child placement materials, collated as part of the BAAF's good practice guide for parent and child fostering (Adams and Dibben, 2011). Parent and child placements require foster carers to work closely and effectively with a range of professionals, in line with the care plans for the parent (where relevant) and the child.

The review meeting itself offers the opportunity for all involved to assess whether or not Becky and Stan can work in line with Bronwyn's and Crystal's care plans, and to consider if parent and child placements are something that they should, and want to, continue to offer. Becky and Stan have done some excellent foster care in the past, but parent and child foster care may or may not be for them.

The RO's report

Having chaired the review, the RO completes their report, which is incorporated into the review documentation submitted to the fostering service and/or the fostering panel. The RO's report provides evidence of their analysis and synthesis of all the material that has been presented for the foster carer review. The report must draw from the review paperwork prepared before the review meeting, and the content of the review meeting itself. The RO, at the end of the report, makes a recommendation about the continuing approval of a foster carer and their terms of approval.

The RO's report evaluates the quality of a foster carer's fostering. The report should differentiate between fact and opinion, and state specifically where information they are utilising in the report is drawn from, i.e. from the review paperwork prepared prior to the review meeting, from what was said in the review meeting or from their own observations in the meeting.

Having read the review paperwork and chaired the review meeting, the RO might have specific matters they wish to comment on regarding the SSW's or the fostering service's practice. For example, they would need to comment if it had become apparent that the SSW visited the foster carer regularly, but had not supervised the work of the foster carer, but rather had developed a relationship more akin to friendship than a professional working relationship. Or, the RO might think that the fostering service's practice contributed to a newly approved foster carer's difficulties by placing three troubled young people with them, leading to one placement ending chaotically. Independence from the fostering service can help the RO make such observations. If the RO is drawn from the fostering service they ought to have a level of seniority, or a role that enables them to make apposite comments in their report.

The structure of the RO's report varies across the UK, as do other reports completed for foster carer reviews. Whatever the structure, it should provide a properly evidenced, holistic, balanced evaluation of the quality of the foster carer's practice. The strengths of the foster carer need to be identified, and there should be examples of what they have done well, as well as any concerns and areas identified for further development.

The final section of the RO report sets out the recommendation about the foster carer's continuing approval and their terms of approval, with a rationale given for both. The RO might make additional recommendations, as was suggested in the Wakefield Inquiry, regarding particular matters. *The review could then have stipulated that there should be no further children placed with them until the matter was resolved* (Parrott et al., 2007, p83).

In requiring excellent foster care for foster children we must remember that foster carers are human and fallible, as are we all, and that they and their families will experience changes of circumstances or particular difficulties, as all families do over time. This might mean that an RO recommends in addition to a foster carer's continuing approval, and terms of approval, particular requirements appropriate to the foster carer's circumstances. For example: that no foster child is placed for the next three months to enable a foster carer to settle into their new home and complete building work on their attic extension; or that no foster children are placed until the foster carer's own child's educational needs are met within their new school; or that no further foster children are placed until work is undertaken with the fostering couple about how caring for foster children impacts on the quality of their relationship, and what the implications are of this on their care of foster children; or that the care of their own learning disabled son's new baby is planned and settled before another foster child is placed into their already busy fostering family. Recommending that no further foster children are placed with a foster carer is not necessarily a criticism of them, or their fostering ability, but can be a realistic appraisal of what can be reasonably expected of a foster carer. Sometimes foster carers need to focus on their family members' needs and/or the foster children that are currently placed with them.

Chapter summary

- For foster carers' reviews to be meaningful and for informed, safe recommendations to be made regarding whether or not a foster carer should continue to foster there needs to be sufficient breadth of contributions. SSWs and their fostering services should give enough time to the process of gathering review reports from contributors, and make sure that the SSWs' evaluative reports are well evidenced, and that their conclusions and recommendations flow logically from the analysis within the reports.

- The foster carer review meeting offers the opportunity for the foster carer, SSW and RO to consider, in detail and in depth, the quality of the fostering that has been done during a review period, thus enabling an evaluation to be made of the quality of that foster care.

- The review meeting is where differences of view, concerns and areas for further development can be explicitly discussed, and plans made about how they will be addressed.

- The review meeting is a forum in which a foster carer's work can be appraised, and where examples of good and excellent work can be identified.

- The foster carer review is the quality assurance mechanism by which the foster carer's central role in a foster child's lived experience of corporate parenting is evaluated. Its significance and importance as part of maintaining good quality experiences for foster children cannot be over-emphasised.

FURTHER READING

Brown, HC (2011) *Good Practice Guide to Foster Carer Reviews: Process, Practicalities and Best Practice.* London: British Association for Adoption and Fostering.

This is a useful comprehensive best-practice guide to foster carer reviews.

Chapter 8
Fostering panels

CHAPTER OBJECTIVES

By the end of this chapter, readers should:

- be familiar with the functions, role and responsibilities of fostering panels;
- understand some of the complex debates that social workers are involved with in their contributions to fostering panels;
- appreciate how our involvement with fostering panels can be further developed.

Introduction

Fostering panels' purpose, process and effectiveness, like foster carer reviews, have attracted surprisingly little scholarly and research curiosity or attention. It is surprising because it is generally assumed, and accepted, that fostering panels act as a cornerstone for the quality assurance of individual foster carer approvals, reviews and foster care provision more generally; yet this assumption has not been interrogated. An inordinate amount of resources are deployed to support and service fostering panels but, thus far, we know little about whether or not they make a difference to the quality of foster care, and in turn the lives of foster children. Indeed, while writing this book it became apparent that the lived experience of social work and foster care, what social workers and foster carers actually do together, such as placement planning meetings, fostering panels, foster carer reviews and SSW supervision of foster carers, has, in the main, escaped the gaze of academics and researchers. In my view, the reason why this lack of academic notice is of interest is that these are the very areas of social work and fostering day-to-day practice that potentially can make a difference to the quality of foster care and foster children's lives, by improving and building upon capable social work and foster care practice.

Regarding fostering panels, there are a few exceptions to this seeming lack of interest, the main one being the BAAF good practice guide on effective fostering panels (Borthwick and Lord, 2011). Although this is not a publication about research findings, it draws together best practice from across the UK, and links it to what is expected of fostering services by Regulation and Guidance, in respect of fostering panels' roles, responsibilities and functions. The guide helpfully sets out all matters relating to fostering panels, the role of the fostering panel chair, adviser and administrator, and clarifies how fostering panels can work in line with national Regulations and Guidance, and what is considered best practice. Borthwick and Lord's book starts with the claim that, *fostering panels have a crucial role to play in the provision and monitoring of foster care for children* (2011, p1), reflecting what most people believe to be the case but, as noted above, a belief that remains unproven; an area of fostering services' function and practice that might benefit from research evaluation.

The current lack of research evidence about fostering panels' usefulness leaves fostering panels, fostering services, foster carers and potentially foster children vulnerable to ideologically fuelled hostility to their existence. One internet blog reads *one reform that would be positive would be the abolition of Adoption Panels. Also the Fostering Panels which have an equivalent role in wasting time and money* (Local Government @ Conservative Home, 2013).

Effective fostering panels, in my experience, can act as a helpful forum, adding a layer of independent scrutiny to decisions and related recommendations being made, that have profound effects on foster carers and foster children. Panels can, in addition, be a moderating and mediating force, ensuring that foster carers are given a transparent, lawful, reasonable and proportionate experience of approval and review processes and, where applicable, the termination of their approval.

This chapter covers

- The regulatory framework for fostering panels

- Foster carers, SSWs and ROs attending fostering panels

- Approvals

- Matching

- Reviews.

What the Standards, Guidance and Regulations say

The Guidance and Regulation in respect of fostering panels are found in:

- The NMS (Department of Education, 2011a, Standard 14, pp30–1);

- The Children Act 1989 Guidance and Regulations Volume 4: Fostering Services (HM Government, 2011, 5.1–5.25, pp38–43);

- The Fostering Service (England) Regulations (Department of Education, 2011b, Regulation 23–25, pp12–14);

- Assessment and Approval of Foster Carers: Amendments to the Children Act 1989 Guidance and Regulations (Department of Education, 2013b).

The Regulations state the functions of the fostering panel as:

> *25. – (1) The functions of the fostering panel in respect of cases referred to it by the Fostering Service provider are –*

(a) to consider each application for approval and to recommend whether or not a person is suitable to be a foster parent,

(b) where it recommends approval of an application, to recommend terms on which the approval is to be given,

(c) to recommend whether or not a person remains suitable to be a foster parent, and whether or not the terms of their approval (if any) remain appropriate –

(i) on the first review carried out in accordance with regulation 28(2), and

(ii) on the occasion of any other review, if requested to do so by the Fostering Service provider in accordance with regulation 28(5), and

(d) to consider any case referred to it under regulation 27(9) or 28(10).

(Department of Education, 2011b, Regulation 25.1, p13)

The fostering panel also has a quality assurance role more generally as follows:

25. – (4) The fostering panel must also –

(a) advise, where appropriate, on the procedures under which reviews in accordance with regulation 28 are carried out by the Fostering Service provider, and periodically monitor their effectiveness,

(b) oversee the conduct of assessments carried out by the Fostering Service provider, and

(c) give advice, and make recommendations, on such other matters or cases as the Fostering Service provider may refer to it.

(Department of Education, 2011b, Regulation 25.4, p13)

The quality assurance deliberations of panels are recorded, and communicated to the fostering service through: the minutes of each panel; the chair's discussions with the ADM; and the fostering panel annual report, recording as it does the work of the panel, and quality assurance matters that have arisen during the course of the preceding year.

A fostering panel's functions are to consider: assessment reports for prospective foster carers; the review paperwork for foster carers; for some fostering services, permanence matching reports for foster carers and named children; and any other matters the fostering service wants it to consider. There is debate about whether fostering panels should comment on matters related to foster children, and their care plans. The main focus of fostering panels should be foster carers. However, this becomes more complex with family and friends foster carer (connected persons) approvals, and matching recommendations for named children with a specific foster carer. The Guidance states: *Panels . . . play an important quality assurance role, providing objectivity and having the ability to challenge practice which is felt to fall short of the Regulations or NMS, or not to be in the interest of children* (HM Government, 2011, 5.2, p38). In this section of the Guidance the fostering panel's brief is understood to include consideration of foster children. It is the fostering panel chair's role to exercise their professional judgement and discernment regarding keeping the fostering panel to task, specific to foster carers, and only commenting on other matters when this is considered necessary, and lies within the expectations set for fostering panels, established through Guidance and Regulation.

Chapter 5 of the Government's Guidance (HM Government, 2011) is dedicated to fostering panels, and matters relevant to fostering panels' functions and responsibilities. The fostering service is required to keep a central list of fostering panel members, which has to include an independent chair and a vice chair, and, for a panel to be quorum, at least one independent member has to be present at every panel meeting, which means that the central list usually is comprised of several independent members, and one or more social workers, with a minimum of three years' post-qualifying experience. The panel membership should reflect a variety of experiences of fostering, including that of a foster carer, a person who has been fostered, education, short breaks care and family and friends care, be gender balanced and reflect the diversity of the local community (HM Government, 2011, 5.8, p39). Fostering panel members are appraised annually, normally by the panel adviser and chair. The independent fostering panel chair is appraised annually too, by the fostering service ADM (HM Government, 2011, 5.15, p41).

The NMS state that the chair of the fostering panel *ensures written minutes of panel meetings are accurate, clearly cover the key issues and views expressed by panel members, and record the reasons for its recommendation* (Department of Education, 2011a, 14.7, p31). The NMS reads as follows:

> *The Fostering Service provider's decision-maker makes a considered decision that takes account of all the information available to them, including the recommendation of the fostering panel and, where applicable, the independent review panel, within seven working days of receipt of the recommendation and final set of panel minutes.*

> (Department of Education, 2011a, 14.7, p31)

This means that the production, checking and agreeing of fostering panel minutes needs to be efficient, and happen in a very short period of time.

The inquiry reports, covered in Chapter 3, raised a number of concerning matters about how fostering services' panels, or panel processes, had not worked as they should have done to safeguard foster children. The relationship between fostering panels and foster carer reviews was noted within the Wakefield (Parrott *et al.*, 2007) and Rotherham (Rotherham Safeguarding Children Board, 2009) reports. In the latter report, review paperwork went to the fostering panel without a review meeting being conducted with the foster carers. The Derbyshire and Nottinghamshire report (Derbyshire and Nottinghamshire County Councils and the Southern Derbyshire and Nottinghamshire District Health Authorities, 1990) noted the lack of accurate minute taking about decisions made by the fostering panel.

SSWs will, in the course of their work, attend many fostering panels as assessors of prospective foster carers, when their foster carer is being reviewed or when a foster child is being matched for permanence with a particular foster carer. In respect of this Lawson writes:

It is important that supervising social workers understand about fostering panels because they play a very important quality assurance role, bringing objectivity into the decision-making process and introducing a degree of independence for the fostering service.

(Lawson, 2011b, p118)

Foster carers, SSWs and ROs attending fostering panels

In the spirit of working in partnership, valuing the contribution that foster carers can make to improve the quality of a foster child's life and inclusivity, foster carers and prospective foster carers should be invited to fostering panels, when their review or approval documentation is being considered. In the case of foster carer reviews, the foster carer, the SSW and the RO will have written evaluative reports for the purposes of the review, and need to attend the fostering panel to answer questions that might arise from the panel's scrutiny of the review documentation, and the related recommendation. In the case of approvals, again the assessor and the prospective foster carer have to be at the panel to support the arguments presented in the paperwork, answer questions that arise from the fostering panel's discussions and defend the recommendation being put to the fostering panel.

It is not uncommon for social work assessors, prospective foster carers, SSWs, foster carers and ROs to find attending fostering panels intimidating. Lawson notes that *even though fostering panels have no decision-making powers, they are often viewed as quite powerful bodies because of the influence that they have* (2011b, p118). It is, therefore, part of the chair's responsibility to: explain the fostering panel process to those attending; introduce everyone; and make sure that the panel's deliberations are well organised, clear and facilitative.

The independent chair should check that the foster carer feels welcomed to the fostering panel, and ensures they are treated in a respectful manner throughout the fostering panel process. Anxiety experienced by foster carers and prospective foster carers attending fostering panels can be mitigated, to some degree, through the respect shown to them by the fostering panel chair and members. Mehmet addresses this, for foster carers, when she writes: *It can be daunting to enter a room where there can be up to ten people waiting to see you, however it is a clear responsibility of any panel, especially the Chair, to make your attendance as comfortable as possible* (2005, p22). It is incumbent upon the fostering panel chair to thank all the contributors for the work they have done in preparing the approval, matching or review documentation, and summarise the strengths of the paperwork and recommendation, as well as identify gaps where they exist.

Fostering services have varying practices for people attending fostering panels, regarding who comes into the fostering panel meeting room and when. It is now common practice for prospective foster carers to attend fostering panels for approval, and foster carers to attend for matching discussions and reviews. This is an improved area of practice, and potentially enhances the fostering panel's thinking, supporting their recommendation. However, sometimes the social work assessor and prospective foster carer, in the case of

131

approvals, or the foster carer and SSW, in the case of foster carer matching and reviews, might have fundamentally different views regarding the recommendation the social work assessor or SSW is proposing to the fostering panel. Fostering panels that see the social work assessor or SSW first, and the prospective foster carer or foster carer after, as well as together, allow for different views to be articulated, shared and explored.

Approvals

The fostering panel's, like the fostering service's, primary responsibility is to foster children. This obvious assertion can sometimes be obscured in the workings of fostering panels, and in assessment reports presented to fostering panels, when the balance shifts too far towards those involved wanting a particular person or couple to be approved as foster carers. Social work assessors, as noted in Chapter 4, inevitably, and rightly, form close working relationships with people they assess, and sometimes that closeness can impinge on their professional judgement. Improving the lives of foster children is the purpose of foster care; it is not an activity designed to meet the needs of those wanting to be foster carers, when they realistically will not be able to assume the many roles and meet the responsibilities that will be required of them. It is equally the case that on occasion a social work assessor might form a negative view about a prospective foster carer, based on their own personal opinion, rather than professional social work knowledge informing their social work assessment. In such cases the fostering panel, where this has not been identified by the social work assessor's manager, can have a moderating influence, and recommend that additional work is undertaken so that a balanced, and professionally informed, recommendation can then be presented to the fostering panel.

The fostering panel's job, regarding prospective foster carer approvals, is to: consider the prospective foster carer assessment paperwork; make sure that all the regulatory requirements for foster carer assessments have been met, including statutory checks and receipt of references; check that the information about the foster carer and their circumstances has been thoroughly analysed, within the report; and that the social work assessor's recommendation is congruent with the content of, and arguments presented within, the body of the report. The fostering panel, having considered the assessment paperwork, and spoken with the social work assessor and the prospective foster carer, is then in a position to make its own recommendation to the fostering service ADM. Borthwick and Lord write: *The panel's role is to examine the assessment report and to consider whether there is evidence of an applicant's abilities and suitability to foster* (2011, p24). However tempting on occasions it is, it is not the role of, nor is it appropriate for, the fostering panel to try to in effect reassess the applicant during the fostering panel meeting.

However good the quality of the assessment paperwork presented to the fostering panel, there will inevitably be some remaining questions, or points for clarification, arising from the paperwork that the fostering panel members will want to discuss with the prospective foster carer, and their social work assessor. Nonetheless, if the assessment paperwork has too many gaps, or themes arising that the fostering panel members think have not been adequately explored in the assessment itself, in such cases, to enable the fostering panel to make a safe enough recommendation regarding whether or not someone should be approved as a foster carer, the recommendation would need to be deferred, for further work to be done by the social work assessor and the foster carer. In such a case the fostering panel would feed back their concerns to the fostering service, because deferring decisions as a result of inadequate assessments is not in the prospective foster carer's, the social work assessor's or the fostering service's interests.

Approval of family and friends foster carers

Approval of 'mainstream' foster carers and the approval of family and friends foster carers (connected persons) can raise different issues for fostering panels. The approval of family and friends foster carers is an area of fostering panel practice that takes fostering panels explicitly into the territory of childcare decision making, and related recommendations. Lawson's book, written for foster carers, is useful for SSWs and children's social workers, as well as panel members, regarding family and friends foster care (2011c). In addition to considering the suitability of the prospective family and friends foster carer to foster, the fostering panel, like the social work assessor and the child's social worker, is addressing the question of whether or not they think a placement with the prospective family and friends foster carer is in a particular child's or children's interests. Usually what is being considered by the fostering panel is the child's/children's long-term interests, because such placements are often being debated in the context of court proceedings, where the intention is permanence for the child, or children, through being placed with their family and friends foster carer until they reach adulthood.

Chapter 5 of the Family and Friends Care: Statutory Guidance for Local Authorities (Department of Education, 2010a, p31) covers the areas to be considered in the assessment and approval of family and friends foster carers, over and above what would be required within 'mainstream' foster carer assessments. The Guidance suggests specific areas that should be covered in the assessment including: family relationships and safeguarding the child; timing of, and attitude towards, the assessment; motivation and impact on the family; carers' own feelings; accommodation; location; health; and parenting capacity. Although some of these areas are the same as those considered for 'mainstream' foster carers, there will be nuanced differences. For example, as noted above, the presentation of assessment reports for approval of family and friends foster carers to fostering panels often runs concurrently with care planning and care proceedings happening for a child. The urgency of such cases, and the related dynamics for all those involved, might therefore be very different from those involved when assessing a 'mainstream' foster carer who will care for children as yet unknown to them.

In addition, the prospective family and friends foster carers' relationship with those with parental responsibility for a child that is either already placed or will be placed with a prospective family and friends foster carer is important for the social work assessor to understand and explore in the assessment report, as this relationship will impact on future contact arrangements for, and safeguarding of, the foster child.

> *Fundamental to the assessment of a relative or friend to be a foster carer will be consideration of the carer's capacity to provide a level of parenting to meet the child's particular needs within the requirements of the care plan, including the placement plan. The child's core assessment and care plan will have identified his or her developmental needs, and the carer's parenting capacity should*

be assessed in relation to those dimensions as described in the Assessment Framework. Family and friends foster carers must be in a position to meet the child's assessed needs, bearing in mind that those needs will often be greater than for other non-looked after children of a similar age. The circumstances of the child's own parents should be identified and the likely impact on the capacity of the family member or friend to provide adequate care assessed.

(Department of Education, 2010a, p39)

The complexity of decision making regarding family and friends foster care, for children, was evidenced in Hunt, Waterhouse and Lutman's research study: *Our conclusions from the project can be simply stated: kinship care can be a positive option for many children but it is not straightforward and requires careful assessment and adequate support* (2008, p296). Fostering panels have to carefully consider if a family and friends foster carer can, and their particular circumstances will, allow them to meet the needs of a particular child or children, and safeguard them during the whole of their childhoods. It is important to note the findings of Farmer and Moyers' research study, looking at family and friends foster care, to make sure that fostering panels do not become over risk averse, and inadvertently make recommendations that are not in children's long-term interest. They found that:

Children placed with family and friends do as well as those with unrelated foster carers but have the important advantage that their placements last longer. Placements with kin generally ensure that children thrive, are well nurtured and remain connected to their roots. These placements therefore deliver good quality and make a major contribution to stability for children who cannot live with their parents.

(Farmer and Moyers, 2008, p236)

Although Farmer and Moyers' research findings were positive overall, it is important to remember that each child, and each family's situation, is different and they have to be examined carefully in their own right. A family and friends placement might be right for one child, but not for another. Fostering panel members should hold in mind that research findings are about the general, and that social work and fostering panel recommendations, in the case of prospective family and friends approvals, are about particular children and prospective foster carers. What Sellick and Thoburn wrote some time ago is still as relevant today:

When it comes to using research to throw light on specific decisions being made about specific children, there is no alternative to a careful scrutiny of the studies which seem most relevant. An appraisal must then be made as to the validity of their conclusions in the context of the specific case.

(Sellick and Thoburn, 1996, p26)

Matching

Many fostering panels now consider the permanent matching of a foster child or children with a specific foster carer. Analogous to family and friends foster carer assessment reports scrutinised by fostering panels, this takes the fostering panel into the realms of childcare practice, and children's care plans. When permanence matching reports are presented to fostering panels the paperwork normally includes: a child's permanence report; the foster carer's original or updated assessment report; the most recent foster carer's review paperwork; and a matching report. Inescapably this involves panel members carefully reading a large quantity of papers.

CASE STUDY *8.1*

For example, fostering panels might see the paperwork for a sibling group of five, where the recommendation is that they are matched permanently with the foster carers they have lived with for the last two years. In this case the original care plan was that the children be placed for adoption, but when no adoptive placement was found, the local authority returned to court to seek revocation of the Placement Orders for the children (A and S Children v Lancashire County Council, 2012). The children's social worker assessed that in the interceding two years since the children were placed with their foster carers, in what had originally been anticipated as a short-term foster placement while adopters were found, the five children and their foster carers had become attached. It was also observed that the children had strong attachments to one another that were helpful to them, so splitting the siblings was not thought any longer to be an option. The children were thriving in the foster carers' family, and it was recommended, by their social worker and the social worker's manager, that the children's best interests would be best served by them remaining with their current foster carers.

In such cases fostering panel members are presented with a large amount of paperwork pertaining to each of the children, because each individual child's history, relationship with their birth family and foster carers and current circumstances have to be considered. A sibling group of five cannot be assumed to be 'a job lot', but rather are five individuals with unique relationships between themselves, with their foster carers, with their birth family and with others.

Research informing matching decision making

To inform decision making about matching children with foster carers, children's social workers and SSWs have relevant, useful publications to inform their practice about children placed permanently with foster carers (McAuley, 1996; Sinclair, Baker, Lee and Gibbs, 2007; Schofield and Beek, 2008; Schofield and Ward, 2011; Schofield and Ward with Warman, Simmonds and Butler, 2008; Biehal, Ellison, Baker and Sinclair, 2010; Schofield *et al.,* 2012; Boddy, 2013; McSherry, Malet and Weatherall, 2013), in addition to pertinent material covered in the fostering research review literature, noted earlier in the book. Additionally, publications about working with families whose children are placed in foster care (Schofield and Ward, 2011) and contact in permanent placements (Neil and Howe, 2004; Adams, 2012; Austerberry *et al.,* 2013) can inform planning for a foster child's contact with their birth family, while placed in permanent foster care. This is a pertinent area for SSWs and children's social workers to explore in matching reports submitted to fostering panels, as it invariably is, even when contact has been directed by the court in care proceedings, because it impacts on the foster placement. Foster carers and their SSWs have to understand why contact might, or might not, be in a particular foster child's or children's interests, and foster carers need the emotional and practical capacity, and support and supervision, to work with the contact plan established in a child's care plan.

Reviews

Chapter 7 considered the role of the RO in evaluating the quality of the fostering undertaken by a foster carer in the review period. The RO makes a professional judgement in this evaluation, which informs their recommendation regarding the continuing approval of a foster carer and their terms of approval. Borthwick and Lord state that the *purpose of the review is to provide an appraisal of the carer's abilities and experience of fostering over the year* (2011, p33). The fostering panel provides further scrutiny. The final review paperwork, including the RO's report, the targets they have set for the forthcoming year for the foster carer, their SSW and fostering service and their recommendation, is examined by the fostering panel. The fostering panel process adds another dimension to the necessary rigour needed to make sure that foster children are offered good quality foster care. In my view it is sensible for the RO, who has chaired a foster carer's review, the SSW and foster carer, when their review is considered by the fostering panel, to attend the fostering panel meeting.

The fostering panel should explicitly address the strengths of the foster care practice, any concerns and areas for further development identified in the review documentation; but the panel process should not try to replicate the review meeting content and process. If the fostering panel members think that the foster carer review process has insufficiently dealt with particular areas, and because of that, the fostering panel cannot safely make a recommendation regarding the foster carer's continuing approval, and terms of approval, then the fostering panel recommendation should be to defer the final panel recommendation to a future panel date. If this is the outcome, clear direction needs to be given about what further work the fostering panel recommends should be undertaken, by whom and by when, to enable a final recommendation to be made at a fostering panel as soon as is possible.

Frequency of reviews going to fostering panels

Fostering services differ in the frequency that foster carer reviews are submitted for their fostering panel's consideration. The fostering Regulations state that the fostering service *must on the occasion of the first review under this regulation, and may on any subsequent review, refer their report to the fostering panel for consideration* (Department of Education, 2011b, Regulation 28 (5)). Therefore first reviews of newly approved foster carers have to be presented to fostering panels within a year of the foster carer's approval (Department of Education, 2011b). The Wakefield Inquiry team (Parrott *et al.*, 2007) and Borthwick and Lord (2011) argue for first reviews of newly approved foster carers being conducted within six months of a foster child being placed with a newly approved foster carer.

Borthwick and Lord, writing about the role of fostering panels in relation to foster carer reviews, write:

> *The fostering panel is required to consider the first review of all foster carers . . . This must have taken place within one year of approval . . . In addition the panel may consider subsequent reviews if referred by the fostering service provider. It is also required to advise on procedures about how reviews are carried out and to monitor these.*

(Borthwick and Lord, 2011, p33)

The frequency of when these 'subsequent reviews' are referred to fostering panels varies between fostering services. Some fostering panels see the review paperwork for every foster carer review. Others refer their foster carer reviews, after the first review, to the fostering panel every three years. There is no regulatory requirement for fostering services, after the first review, to submit any subsequent reviews to their fostering panel. However, it is my view that, wherever possible, and if resources allow, fostering panels should see all foster carer reviews, as this allows the panel to have oversight of the ongoing quality of individual foster carers' work, as well as the overall quality of foster care being provided by that fostering service. However, the realities of resource constraints mean that for many fostering services this is not possible. Where this is not possible best practice would suggest that fostering panels see a foster carer's review paperwork every three years as a minimum. Fostering panels in both their regulatory and quality assurance functions need to comment on the proper conduct of reviews. Fostering panels offer a quality assurance role and this role should be exploited by fostering services.

Where there has been a significant change in the foster carer's circumstance, not warranting a new assessment but triggering a review being undertaken, such reviews' paperwork should be seen by the fostering panel. When a review has been undertaken because there are concerns about standards of foster care, or where there has been an allegation made against a foster carer, then again such reviews' paperwork should be scrutinised by the fostering panel.

In Borthwick and Lord's guide to effective fostering panels they suggest the following for when foster carer reviews should come to a fostering panel:

- *For first reviews, panels could consider reviews of new carers at six months and then at one year.*

- *All reviews, where changes of approval are required, could be referred to the panel.*

- *Reviews following child protection concerns or allegations made about standards of care provided by foster carers could be referred to the panel.*

- *Reviews could be referred every three years, even where there is no change, in order to provide some external monitoring and scrutiny of agency and fostering practice.*

(Borthwick and Lord, 2011, p34)

Belfast Metropolitan College

Millfield LRC

When a review is triggered by an investigation into an allegation made against a foster carer, or a standard of care matter has been raised, the RO foster carer review report usefully notes: the strengths of the foster carer and their foster care to date; any historical concerns that have been raised about the foster carer; the detail of the allegation or standard of care matter; the outcome of the final strategy meeting where relevant; and a clear, well-evidenced conclusion and recommendations regarding whether or not the foster carer remains appropriate to be a foster carer; whether or not their household remains a suitable environment for fostering; and if their current terms of approval remain relevant. Such clarity in the RO's report is helpful for the fostering panel when the panel members come to make their own recommendation about whether or not the foster carer should continue to be approved, what their terms of approval should be and any other matters that they think might be relevant.

Paperwork submitted to fostering panels

The review paperwork submitted to the fostering panel should be proofread by the SSW, and the fostering service, and signed off by the SSW's manager, as being fit for purpose. The quality of the paperwork presented to fostering panels, whatever the purpose of that paperwork, needs to be checked before being sent to fostering panel members. If the fostering panel chair has any queries or concerns about the paperwork for any case being presented to the next fostering panel, they can raise them with the panel adviser, prior to the fostering panel, in sufficient time for matters to be, wherever possible, resolved prior to the fostering panel meeting. Social workers' paperwork presented to fostering panels needs to be fluent, concise and analytical, as discussed in the previous chapter. This enables fostering panel members to be conversant with the facts of the case, and understand the arguments being presented, that lead to a logically argued, and clearly evidenced recommendation.

The review paperwork as noted in Chapter 7 as required by regulation must include:

- the SSW's report;
- the foster carer's input;
- the views of all foster children placed with the foster carer;
- the views of foster children's social workers for all foster children placed with the foster carer either from the time of their approval, if they are a newly approved foster carer, or since their last review.

In addition I have argued that best practice would dictate that the following ought to be added to this list:

- the views of all foster children that have been in placement during the review period but have moved on;
- the foster carer's own children's views;
- the foster children's parents' views (where this is appropriate);
- third-party views – for example from a foster child's school, nursery, health visitor, Youth Offending Service, etc.

Fostering services collate their foster carer review paperwork for fostering panel purposes in different ways, and each will have a rationale. Whatever way the review papers are collated, there needs to be a logical sequencing of reports for each foster carer's review being sent to the fostering panel members for them to be able to understand what is being presented and its significance. Fostering panel members need to receive the paperwork a minimum of five working days before a fostering panel meeting, and wherever possible earlier, to give them plenty of time to read the review documentation, and prepare for the fostering panel meeting.

Fostering panel recommendations when considering foster carer reviews

Having securitised the review paperwork and had the opportunity to ask questions for clarification to the foster carer, the SSW and the RO, the fostering panel members should be in a position to make a recommendation to the ADM. The fostering service ADM makes the final decision informed by the review documentation, and the deliberations of the fostering panel are recorded in the panel minutes, about whether or not a foster carer should continue to be approved, and what their terms of approval should be. In line with the Regulations this decision needs to be given to the foster carer in writing (Department of Education, 2011b; Department of Education, 2013b). Where the panel is recommending a change to the foster carer's terms of approval, and the foster carer is in agreement with this recommendation, the rationale for this change and the foster carer's agreement, and any related support needs and how these will be met, should be noted in the fostering panel minutes.

Where an RO and/or an SSW recommend that a foster carer's approval is terminated and/or their terms of approval changed but the foster carer is not in agreement with the recommendation, then the panel process outlined in Borthwick and Lord's effective fostering panels publication is usually followed by fostering services (2011, pp35–6). The foster carer *should have read this report and should have been invited to provide their own observations in writing for the panel to consider* (Borthwick and Lord, 2011, p36). In such circumstances the situation necessitates that the foster carer be advised that they might want to bring a support person with them because their attendance at the fostering panel is likely to be stressful. The attendance of a support person is normally agreed by the fostering service, and the chair of the fostering panel. Where a foster carer does bring a supporter, the chair needs to explain their role in supporting the foster carer but not speaking for them. Where a foster carer brings a solicitor with them the chair needs to explain to both the foster carer and the solicitor that the solicitor is there in the role of a support person, not as a legal representative (Borthwick and Lord, 2011, p36).

If the fostering panel decides to recommend to the fostering service ADM that the foster carer is no longer suitable to foster, or that their terms of approval be changed, where the foster carer is not in agreement with this recommendation this needs to be explained orally to the foster carer by the fostering panel chair, as does the subsequent process including their potential recourse to the Independent Review Mechanism (Department of Education, 2013b). The minute taker for the fostering panel should record that this was done.

Where the fostering panel recommends to the fostering service that the foster carer's approval be terminated, or that their terms of approval are changed and the foster carer is not in agreement, and the fostering service ADM is in agreement with this recommendation, Regulation (Department of Education, 2011b, 7–15, p28) and recent Guidance has to be followed (Department of Education, 2013b, p15). The ADM sends the foster carer a 'qualifying determination', written notice of the proposed decision, explains why the decision has been made and advises that they have 28 days in which to make representation to the ADM, or apply to the Secretary of State for their case to be considered by the Independent Review Mechanism (Lawson, 2011b, p127).

Chapter summary

- Fostering panels' scrutiny of foster carer approval, matching and review documentation and assessors', children's social workers' and SSWs' recommendations adds another dimension to the necessary rigour that should be deployed when informing a fostering service's ADM's decision making about a foster carer's approval, children being matched permanently with a foster carer and a foster carers' continuing approval, and terms of approval.

- Foster carers undertake complex, invaluable work with foster children within their own homes. Attendance at foster panels, when their review paperwork is being considered, although usually anxiety provoking, can be an affirming experience. It is a forum in which their contributions to the lives of specific foster children, and to the wider community, can be recognised.

- This recognition of foster carers', prospective foster carer assessors' and SSWs' work, by the fostering service, is important.

- Fostering panel members have to hold in mind that their primary responsibility is to foster children. The UKNSFC Standard 23.2 notes that *The panel's terms of reference stress a primary responsibility to act in the best interest of children and young people placed in foster care by the authority* (UK Joint Working Party on Foster Care, 1999a, p62). The welfare of foster children has to be fostering panels' paramount consideration in line with the Children Act 1989.

FURTHER READING

Borthwick, S and Lord, J (2011) *Effective Fostering* Panels, 3rd edition. London: BAAF.

At the time of writing this text remained the most comprehensive publication about fostering panels.

Chapter 9
Conclusion

Foster care can make a profound beneficial difference to the lives of children in public care. Social workers in the field of foster care assess, support, supervise and help develop foster carers, enabling them and contributing to them making positive changes for children and young people for whom they care.

Social workers, working with foster carers, need the generic knowledge, values and skills that are required by all social workers to practise capably, in any area of social work, whether it is mental health, working within palliative care, child protection or in youth justice. As with all specialist areas of practice, in addition to the generic social work knowledge, values and skills, in the field of fostering, social workers have to be research literate and informed about foster care and children looked after. Practitioners need to be fully conversant with the legal and policy framework for fostering, within which their social work with foster carers takes place. Findings and recommendations from SCRs and inquiry reports, relevant to foster care, act as case studies from which we can learn and build our practice.

This book examined social work and foster care in relation to: recruitment and assessment; supervision and support; training and development; reviews; and panels. Each chapter drew on what we know from existing research evidence, where there is such evidence, and from best practice guidance. To remain effective as social workers, as part of our continuing professional development, we need to keep abreast of developments in policy, regulation, guidance and research; we owe that to foster carers, foster children and their families.

At the time of writing The College of Social Work was consulting with various parties regarding the development of a specialist capability statement for adoption and fostering. Both the professional capability framework, designed by the Social Work Reform Board, and taken on by The College of Social Work, and the Standards of Proficiency for Social Work, created by the Health and Care Professions Council, both generic, have been mapped against each other (The College of Social Work, 2012). However, the intention is that the new specialist capability statements specific to social work in fostering and adoption *will set out how social workers in adoption and fostering should evidence their capability against the PCF in this specialist area of work, from their first year in employment through to senior strategic roles* (Patel, 2013, p2). We will have to wait and see what these statements comprise, and if this College of Social Work development ultimately positively affects the life chances of fostered and adopted children, which will be the most important measure of their usefulness.

Foster care is currently, and is likely to remain within the foreseeable future, the foremost type of 'accommodation' for and intervention in the lives of children who are looked after. It is therefore of great importance that, as social workers and foster carers, we garner collective passion and commitment to make sure that foster care is as warm, caring and effective in meeting children's and young people's emotional, educational, leisure and health needs as it can be. Foster care can be, and often is, the site of reparatory intervention, somewhere a child can recover and move forward with hope. We have a responsibility to those children to make sure that their experience of foster care is as good as it possibly can be, providing the chance of, as well as recovery, fun, stimulation, new experiences, manageable boundaries, helpful routine, nourishment in all its forms, warmth and love. As with all families, foster family life is also the space where children and young people can learn to manage disappointment, anger, frustration, loss and transition. Foster care is care of children in a safe family environment, where they can learn how to live within a family that is organised well enough, and one that is committed to them.

For foster carers to provide the level of care to children that we expect of them, they have to feel valued, supported and cared for themselves by society, their fostering service and their SSWs. I have argued that social work has a key role in providing support and supervision to foster carers, to make sure that they are as effective as they can be. Foster carers and social workers together can make a difference to foster children's lives.

References

A and S v Lancs CC [2012] EWHC 1689 (Fam).

Adams, P (2012) *Planning for Contact in Permanent Placements*. London: BAAF.

Adams, P and Dibben, E (2011) *Parent and Child Fostering*. London: BAAF.

All Wales Child Protection Procedures Review Group (2011) *Safeguarding and Promoting the Welfare of Unaccompanied Asylum Seeking Children and Young People, All Wales Practice Guidance*. Cardiff: All Wales Child Protection Procedures Review Group.

Argent, H and Coleman, J (2012) *Dealing with Disruptions in Fostering and Adoption Placements*. London: BAAF.

Aspinwall-Roberts, A (2012) *Assessments in Social Work with Adults*. Maidenhead: Open University Press.

Austerberry, H, Stanley, N, Larkins, C, Ridley, J, Farrelly, N, Manthorpe, J and Hussein, S (2013) Foster carers and family contact: foster carers' views of social work support. *Adoption and Fostering*, 37(2): 116–29.

Bachmann, K, Blackeby, K, Bengo, C, Slack, K, Woolgar, M, Lawson, H and Scott, S (2011) *Fostering Changes: How to Improve Relationships and Manage Difficult Behaviour: A Training Programme for Foster Carers*. London: BAAF.

Barn, R and Kirton, D (2012) Transracial adoption in Britain: politics, ideology and reality. *Adoption and Fostering*, 36(3,4): 25–37.

Beckett, C (2010) *Assessment and Intervention in Social Work: Preparing for Practice*. London: Sage.

Beesley, P (2010) *Making Good Assessments: A Practical Resource Guide*. London: BAAF.

Berridge, D (1997) *Foster Care: A Research Review*. London: TSO.

Berridge, D (2012) Educating young people in care: what have we learned? *Children and Youth Services Review*, 34: 1171–5.

Biehal, N (2013) Maltreatment in foster care: a review of the evidence. *Child Abuse Review*, Wiley Online Library, doi: 10.1002/car.2249.

Biehal, N and Parry, E (2010) *Maltreatment and Allegations of Maltreatment in Foster Care: A Review of the Evidence*. York: The University of York Social Policy Research Unit/London: The Fostering Network.

Biehal, N, Ellison, S, Baker, C and Sinclair, I (2010) *Belonging and Permanence Outcomes in Long-Term Foster Care and Adoption*. London: BAAF.

Biehal, N, Dixon, J, Parry, E and Sinclair, I (University of York); Green, J, Roberts, C, Kay, C, Rothwell, J, Kapadia, D and Roby, A (University of Manchester) (2012) *The Care Placement Evaluation (CaPE) Evaluation of Multidimensional Treatment Foster Care for Adolescents (MTFC-A)*. London: Department of Education.

Boddy, J (2013) *Understanding Permanence for Looked After Children: A Review of Research for the Care Inquiry*. London: Nuffield Foundation.

Borthwick, S and Lord, J (2011) *Effective Fostering Panels* (3rd edition). London: BAAF.

Brammer, A (2010) *Social Work Law* (3rd edition). Harlow: Pearson Education Ltd.

Brandon, M, Bailey, S and Belderson, P (2010) *Building on the Learning from Serious Case Reviews: A Two-Year Analysis of Child Protection Notifications, 2007–2009.* London: Department of Education.

Brandon, M, Sidebotham, P, Bailey, S, Belderson, P, Hawley, C, Ellis, C and Megson, M (2012) *New Learning from Serious Case Reviews: A Two-Year Report for 2009–2011.* London: Department of Education.

Brayne, H and Carr, H (2013) *Law for Social Workers.* Oxford: Oxford University Press.

Briskman, J, Castle, J, Blackeby, K, Bengo, C, Slack, K, Stebbens, C, Leaver, W and Scott, S (2012) *Randomised Controlled Trial of the Fostering Changes Programme.* London: National Academy for Parenting Research/London: King's College/Department of Education.

British Association for Adoption and Fostering Assessment Working Party (1998) *Preparing for Permanence. Key Issues in Assessment: Points to Address during the Assessment Process.* London: BAAF.

British Association for Adoption and Fostering (2008) *Prospective Foster Carer(s) Report (Form F).* London: BAAF.

British Association for Adoption and Fostering (2012) Multiculturalism, identity and family placement, in Phoenix, A and Simmonds, J (eds) *Adoption and Fostering,* 36(3,4): 1–143.

British Association for Adoption and Fostering (2013a) *Statistics: England.* London: BAAF, www.baaf. org.uk/res/statengland

British Association for Adoption and Fostering (2013b) *Form FR.* London: BAAF.

Brown, HC (1991) Competent child-focused practice: working with lesbian and gay carers. *Adoption and Fostering,* 15(2): 11–17.

Brown, HC (2008) Social work and sexuality, working with lesbians and gay men: what remains the same and what is different. *Practice: Social Work in Action,* 20(4): 265–76.

Brown, HC (2011) *Good Practice Guide to Foster Carer Reviews: Process, Practicalities and Best Practice.* London: BAAF.

Brown, HC (forthcoming) Young lesbians and gay men: survival and agency, in Goodman, A and Kennison, P (eds) *Children as Victims and Survivors.* London: Sage/Learning Matters.

Brown, HC and Cocker, C (2008) Lesbian and gay fostering and adoption: out of the closet into the mainstream. *Adoption and Fostering,* 32(4): 19–30.

Brown, HC and Cocker, C (2011) *Social Work with Lesbians and Gay Men.* London: Sage.

Brown, HC and Kershaw, S (2008) The legal context of working with lesbians and gay men. *Social Work Education,* 27(2): 122–130.

Brown, HC, Fry, E and Howard, J (2005) *How Family Placements Can Keep Children and Families Together.* Lyme Regis: Russell House Publishing.

Caballero, C, Edwards, R, Goodyer, A and Okitikpi, T (2012) The diversity and complexity of the everyday lives of mixed racial and ethnic families: implications for adoption and fostering practice and policy. *Adoption and Fostering,* 36(3 and 4): 9–24.

Cairns, K (2002) *Attachment, Trauma and Resilience: Therapeutic Caring for Children.* London: BAAF.

Cairns, K and Fursland, E (2007) *Safer Caring: A Training Programme.* London: BAAF.

Care Inquiry (2013) *Making Not Breaking: Building Relationships for Our Most Vulnerable Children.* London: The Fostering Network.

Chamberlain, P, Price, J, Leve, LD, Laurent, H, Landsverk, JA and Reid, JB (2008) Prevention of behaviour problems for children in foster care: outcomes and mediation effects. *Prevention Science,* 9: 17–27.

Chapman, R (2009) *Undertaking a Fostering Assessment.* London: BAAF.

Cocker, C and Brown, HC (2010) Sex, sexuality and relationships: developing confidence and discernment when assessing lesbian and gay prospective adopters. *Adoption and Fostering,* 34(1): 20–32.

Cocker, C and Hafford-Letchfield, P (eds) (forthcoming) *Rethinking Anti-discriminatory Practice, Diversity and Equality in Social Work.* Basingstoke: Palgrave/Macmillan.

Corby, B, Doig, A and Roberts, V (2001) *Public Inquiries into Abuse of Children in Residential Care.* London: Jessica Kingsley Publishers.

Coulshed, V and Orme, J (2006) *Social Work Practice.* Basingstoke: Palgrave/Macmillan.

Cree, V and Myers, S (2008) *Social Work: Making a Difference.* Bristol: The Policy Press.

Crump, E (2012) Driver insists overtaking two cars in Mid Wales death crash was 'safe'. *Daily Post,* 30 August 2012, www.dailypost.co.uk/news/north-wales-news/2012/08/30/driver-insists-overtaking-two-cars-in-mid-wales-death-crash-was-safe-55578-31724729

Curtis, Dame M (1946) *Report of the Care of Children Committee,* Cmd 6922. London: HMSO.

Daniel, G (2008) Talking with children: constructing victim-hood or agency, in Kennison, P and Goodman, A (eds) *Children as Victims.* Exeter: Learning Matters, pp91–102.

Davis, L (2010) *A Practical Guide to Fostering Law: Fostering Regulations, Child Care Law and the Youth Justice System.* London: Jessica Kingsley Publishers.

Department for Children, Schools and Families (2009) *Promoting the Health and Well-Being of Looked After Children.* London: Department for Children, Schools and Families.

Department for Children, Schools and Families (2010a) *Short Breaks: Statutory Guidance on How to Safeguard and Promote the Welfare of Disabled Children Using Short Breaks.* London: Department for Children, Schools and Families.

Department for Children, Schools and Families (2010b) *Sufficiency Statutory Guidance on Securing Sufficient Accommodation for Looked After Children.* London: Department for Children, Schools and Families.

Department for Children, Schools and Families (2010c) *Promoting the Educational Achievement of Looked After Children: Statutory Guidance for Local Authorities.* London: Department for Children, Schools and Families.

Department for Children, Schools and Families (2010d) *IRO Handbook: Statutory Guidance for Independent Reviewing Officers and Local Authorities on Their Functions in Relation to Case Management and Review.* London: Department for Children, Schools and Families.

Department of Education (2010a) *Family and Friends Care: Statutory Guidance for Local Authorities.* London: Department of Education.

Department of Education (2010b) *The Children Act 1989 Guidance and Regulations Volume 3: Planning Transition to Adulthood for Care Leavers Including The Care Leavers (England) Regulations 2010.* London: Department of Education.

Department of Education (2011a) *Fostering Services: National Minimum Standards.* London: Department of Education.

Department of Education (2011b) *The Fostering Services (England) Regulations.* London: Department of Education.

Department of Education (2011c) *The Foster Carers' Charter*. London: Department of Education.

Department of Education (2012a) *Improving Fostering Services: Government Proposals*. London: Department of Education, www.education.gov.uk/childrenandyoungpeople/families/fostercare/a00209220/proposals

Department of Education (2012b) *Training, Support and Development Standards for Foster Care, Guidance*. London: Department of Education.

Department of Education (2012c) *Training, Support and Development Standards for Family and Friends Foster Carers, Guidance*. London: Department of Education.

Department of Education (2012d) *Short Break Carers Supplementary Guidance for Managers, Supervisors and Trainers, Training, Support and Development Standards for Short Break Carers*. London: Department of Education.

Department of Education (2012e) *Setting the Standards: Using the Training, Support and Development Standards with Support Carers, Practice Guidance*. London: Department of Education.

Department of Education (2012f) *Training, Support and Development Standards for Foster Care Evidence Workbook*. London: Department of Education.

Department of Education (2013a) *The Care Planning, Placement and Case Review and Fostering Services (England) (Miscellaneous Amendments) Regulations*. London: Department of Education.

Department of Education (2013b) *Assessment and Approval of Foster Carers: Amendments to the Children Act and 1989 Guidance and Regulations, Volume 4: Fostering Services*. London: Department of Education.

Department of Education (2013c) *Delegation of Authority: Amendments to the Children Act 1989 Guidance and Regulations, Volume 2: Care Planning, Placement and Case Review*. London: Department of Education.

Department of Education (2013d) *Fostering Information Exchange*. London: Department of Education, www.education.gov.uk/childrenandyoungpeople/families/fostercare/a00217374/fostering-information-exchange

Department for Education and Skills (2005a) *The Children (Private Arrangements for Fostering) Regulations, No. 1533*. London: DfES.

Department for Education and Skills (2005b) *Replacement Guidance Children Act 1989 Private Fostering*. London: DfES.

Department for Education and Skills (2005c) *National Minimum Standards for Private Fostering*. London: DfES.

Department for Education and Skills (2007) *Care Matters: Time for Change*. Norwich: TSO.

Department of Health (1991) *Child Abuse: A Study of Enquiry Reports, 1980–89*. London: HMSO.

Department of Health (2002) *Fostering Services National Minimum Standards, Fostering Services Regulations*. London: TSO.

Department of Health and Social Service (1999) *Code of Practice on the Recruitment, Assessment, Approval, Training, Management and Support of Foster Carers*. Belfast: Department of Health and Social Service.

Derbyshire and Nottinghamshire County Councils and the Southern Derbyshire and Nottinghamshire District Health Authorities (1990) *Report of the Inquiry into the Death of a Child in Care*. Derby:

Derbyshire and Nottinghamshire County Councils and the Southern Derbyshire and Nottinghamshire District Health Authorities.

Dibben, E (2012) *Devising a Placement Plan: A Guide to Gathering Information to Complete a Placement Plan for Fostering Placements (England)*. London: BAAF.

Dunster, N (2011) *The New Fostering Standards, Regulations and Statutory Guidance (England): What's New? What's Changed?* London: BAAF.

Fahlberg, VI (2008) *A Child's Journey through Placement*. London: BAAF.

Farmer, E and Moyers, S (2008) *Kinship Care: Fostering Effective Family and Friends Placements*. London: Jessica Kingsley Publishers.

Farmer, E, Moyers, S and Lipscombe, J (2004) *Fostering Adolescents*. London: Jessica Kingsley Publishers.

Featherstone, B (2010) Engaging fathers: promoting gender equality?, in Featherstone, B, Hooper, C, Scourfield, J and Taylor, J (eds) *Gender and Child Welfare in Society*. Oxford: Wiley-Blackwell, pp173–84.

Featherstone, B and Green, L (2013) Judith Butler, in Gray, M and Webb, SA (eds) *Social Work Theories and Methods,* 2nd edition. London: Sage, pp63–72.

Ferguson, H (2010) Walks, home visits and atmospheres: risk and everyday practices and mobilities of social work and child protection. *British Journal of Social Work,* 40(4): 1100–17.

Fernandez, C and Dolan, A (2007) Toddler drowned in pool as her foster parents partied. *Mail Online,* 31 July 2007, www.dailymail.co.uk/news/article-471778/Toddler-drowned-pool-foster-parents-partied.html

Forsyth, B (2000) *LGBT Youth and Social Inclusion: A Review of Existing Research*. Edinburgh: Edinburgh Youth Social Inclusion Partnership.

Fursland, E, with Cairns, K and Stanway, C (2013) *Supporting Education*. London: BAAF.

Gilligan, R (2009) *Promoting Resilience*. London: BAAF.

Glendinning, L (2007) Child in foster care dies after being found in swimming pool. *The Guardian,* 31 July 2007, www.guardian.co.uk/society/2007/jul/31/adoptionandfostering.childrensservices

Gloucestershire Safeguarding Children Board (2008) *Executive Summary 0105 Mrs Spry – Version 2.* Gloucestershire: Gloucestershire Safeguarding Children Board.

Gold, D (2005) *Sexual Exclusion: Issues and Best Practice in Lesbian, Gay and Bisexual Housing and Homelessness*. London: Stonewall Housing/Shelter.

Golombok, S (2000) *Parenting: What Really Counts?* London: Routledge.

Goodyer, A (2011) *Child-Centred Foster Care: A Rights-Based Model for Practice*. London: Jessica Kingsley Publishers.

Guasp, A (2012) *The School Report: The Experiences of Gay Young People in Britain's Schools in 2012.* London: Stonewall/Cambridge: University of Cambridge Centre for Family Research.

Guyton, T (2013) *The Heidelberg Art Project,* Detroit, www.heidelberg.org

Hammersmith and Fulham (1984) *Report on the Death of Shirley Woodcock*. London: London Borough of Hammersmith and Fulham.

Harber, A and Oakley, M (2012) *Fostering Aspirations: Reforming the Foster Care System in England and Wales*. London: Policy Exchange.

Harlow, E and Blackburn, F (2011) Fostering matters: a foster carer's perspective, in Harlow, E (ed) *Foster Care Matters.* London: Whiting and Birch Ltd.

Heywood, J (1965) *Children in Care.* London: Routledge and Kegan Paul.

Hicks, S (2011) *Lesbian, Gay, and Queer Parenting: Families, Intimacies, Genealogies.* Basingstoke: Palgrave/Macmillan.

HM Government (2010) *The Children Act Guidance and Regulations, Volume 2: Care Planning, Placement and Case Review.* London: Department for Children, Schools and Families.

HM Government (2011) *The Children Act 1989 Guidance and Regulations, Volume 4: Fostering Services.* London: Department of Education.

HM Government (2013a) *'STAYING PUT': Arrangements for Care Leavers Aged 18 and Above to Stay On with Their Former Foster Carers, Department of Education, DWP and HMRC Guidance.* London: Department of Education.

HM Government (2013b) *Working Together to Safeguard Children: A Guide to Inter-agency Working to Safeguard and Promote the Welfare of Children* (5th edition). London: Department of Education.

Holland, S (2011) *Child and Family Assessment in Social Work Practice* (2nd edition). London: Sage.

Home Office (1933) *The Children and Young Persons (Boarding Out) Rules 1933, Statutory Rules and Orders No 787.* London: Home Office.

Home Office (1945) *Report by Sir Walter Monkton on the Circumstances Which Led to the Boarding Out of Dennis and Terrance O'Neill at Bank Farm, Minsterley and the Steps Taken to Supervise Their Welfare.* London: HMSO.

House of Lords, House of Commons Joint Select Committee on Human Rights (2013) *Human Rights of Unaccompanied Migrant Children and Young People in the UK, First Report of Session 2013–2014, HL Paper 9, HC Paper 196.* London: TSO.

Howe, K and Gray, I (2012) *Effective Supervision in Social Work.* London: Sage/Learning Matters.

Hunt, J, Waterhouse, S and Lutman, E (2008) *Keeping Them in the Family: Outcomes for Children Placed in Kinship Care through Care Proceedings.* London: BAAF.

Husain, F (2006) Cultural competence, cultural sensitivity and family support, in Dolan, P, Canavan, J and Pinkerton, J (eds) *Family Support as Reflective Practice.* London: Jessica Kingsley Publishers, pp165–80.

Laird, SE (2010) *Practical Social Work Law: Analysing Court Cases and Inquiries.* Harlow: Pearson Education Limited.

Laird, SE (2013) *Child Protection: Managing Conflict, Hostility and Aggression.* Bristol: The Policy Press.

Lawson, D (2011a) *Fostering Regulations, Guidance and NMS 2011 (England).* London: The Fostering Network.

Lawson, D (2011b) *A Foster Care Handbook for Supervising Social Workers (England).* London: The Fostering Network.

Lawson, D (2011c) *Family and Friends Foster Care: Information for Foster Carers (England).* London: The Fostering Network.

Le Riche, P and Tanner, K (1998) *Observation and Its Application to Social Work: Rather Like Breathing.* London: Jessica Kingsley Publishers.

Lefevre, M (2010) *Communicating with Children and Young People: Making a Difference.* Bristol: The Policy Press.

Local Government @ Conservative Home (2013) *Adoption and Fostering Panels Should be Scrapped*, http://conservativehome.blogs.com/localgovernment/2013/03/adoption-and-fostering-panels-should-be-scrapped.html

London Evening Standard (2007) *Sadistic Foster Mother's 19-Year Reign of Terror*, www.thisislondon.co.uk/news/articles-23389711

Loughton, T (2012) *Letter Dated 12th June 2012*. London: Department of Education.

Luckock, B and Lefevre, M (2008) *Direct Work: Social Work with Children and Young People in Care.* London: BAAF.

Luke, N and Sebba, J (2013) *How Are Foster Carers Selected? An International Literature Review of Instruments Used within Foster Carers Selection.* Oxford: Rees Centre, University of Oxford.

Mallon, GP and Betts, B (2005) *Recruiting, Assessing and Supporting Lesbian and Gay Carers and Adopters.* London: BAAF.

Martin, R (2010) *Social Work Assessment.* Exeter: Learning Matters.

McAuley, C (1996) *Children in Long-Term Foster Care: Emotional and Social Development.* Aldershot: Avebury.

McDermid, S, Holmes, L, Kirton, D and Signoretta, P (2012) *The Demographic Characteristics of Foster Carers in the UK: Motivations, Barriers and Messages for Recruitment and Retention.* London: Childhood Wellbeing Research Centre.

Mckitterick, B (2012) *Supervision.* Maidenhead: Open University Press.

McSherry, D, Malet, MF and Weatherall, K (2013) *Comparing Long-Term Placements for Young Children in Care: The Care Pathways and Outcomes Study – Northern Ireland.* London: BAAF.

Mehmet, M (2005) *What the Standards Say About Fostering.* Lyme Regis: Russell House Publishing.

Mellish, L, Jennings, S, Tasker, F, Lamb, M and Golombok, S (2013) *Gay, Lesbian and Heterosexual Adoptive Families: Family Relationships, Child Adjustment and Adopters' Experiences.* London: BAAF.

Milner, J and O'Byrne, P (2009) *Assessment in Social Work.* Basingstoke: Palgrave/Macmillan.

Minnis, H, Devine, C and Pelosi, T (1999) Foster carers speak about training. *Adoption and Fostering*, 23(2): 42–7.

Minnis, H, Pelosi, AJ, Knapp, M and Dunn, J (2001) Mental health and foster carer training. *Archives of Disease in Childhood*, 84: 302–6.

Morrison, T and Wonnacott, J (2010) *Supervision: Now or Never. Reclaiming Reflective Supervision in Social Work.* London: Social Work Reform Board, www.education.gov.uk/swrb/employers/a0074263/Standards-for-employers-and-supervision-framework

Multidimensional Treatment Foster Care in England (2013) *KEEP*, www.mtfce.org.uk/keep.html

Munro, E (2008) *Effective Child Protection* (2nd edition). London: Sage.

Munro, E (2011) Munro review of child protection: final report – a child-centred system. London: Department of Education.

National Implementation Team (2008) *Multidimensional Treatment Foster Care in England (MTFCE), Annual Project Report.* London: Department for Children, Schools and Families.

National Implementation Team (2011) *Multidimensional Treatment Foster Care in England, Annual Project Report 2011.* London: MTFCE Implementation Team.

Neil, E and Howe, D (2004) *Contact in Adoption and Permanent Foster Care: Research, Theory and Practice.* London: BAAF.

Nutt, L (2006) *The Lives of Foster Carers: Private Sacrifices, Public Restrictions.* London: Routledge.

Ogilvie, K, Kirton, D and Beecham, J (2006) Foster carer training: resources, payment and support. *Adoption and Fostering,* 30(3): 6–16.

Pallett, C, Scott, S, Blackeby, K, Yule, W and Weissman, R (2002) Fostering changes: a cognitive-behavioural approach to help foster carers manage children. *Adoption and Fostering,* 26(1): 39–48.

Pallett, C, Blackeby, K, Yule, W, Weissman, R and Scott, S (2005) *Fostering Changes: How to Improve Relationships and Manage Difficult Behaviour: A Training Programme for Foster Carers.* London: BAAF.

Parker, J and Bradley, G (2010) *Social Work Practice: Assessment, Planning, Intervention and Review.* Exeter: Learning Matters.

Parrott, B, MacIver, A and Thoburn, J (2007) *Independent Inquiry Report into the Circumstances of Child Sexual Abuse by Two Foster Carers in Wakefield.* Wakefield: Wakefield County Council.

Parton, N (2011) *The Increasing Length and Complexity of Central Government Guidance About Child Protection in England: 1974–2010,* unpublished paper. Huddersfield: University of Huddersfield, http://eprints.hud.ac.uk/9906/

Patel, V (2013) *TCSW Workshops: Drafting Specialist Capability Statements for Adoption and Fostering* (letter dated 20 September 2013). London: College of Social Work.

Patterson, C (2005) *Lesbian and Gay Parenting.* Washington DC: American Psychological Association.

Peake, L (2009) *Caring for Children with Disabilities: The Results of a Consultation on the Learning and Support Needs of the Foster Care Workforce.* London: The Fostering Network.

Peake, L and Townsend, L (2012) *The Motivations to Foster: A Toolkit for Fostering Services.* London: The Fostering Network.

Pithouse, A, Young, C and Butler, I (2002) Training foster carers in challenging behaviour: a case study in disappointment. *Child and Family Social Work,* 7(3): 203–14.

Price, JP, Chamberlain, P, Landsverk, J and Reid, J (2009) KEEP foster-parent training intervention: model description and effectiveness. *Child and Family Social Work,* 14: 233–42.

Reder, P and Duncan, S (2004) From Colwell to Climbié: inquiring into fatal child abuse, in Stanley, N and Manthorpe, J (eds) *The Age of the Inquiry: Learning and Blaming in Health and Social Care.* London: Routledge, pp92–115.

Reder, P, Duncan, S and Gray, M (1993) *Beyond Blame: Child Abuse Tragedies Revisited.* London: Routledge.

Roberts, R, Scott, S and Jones, H (2005) Treatment foster care in England, in Wheal, A (ed) *The RHP Companion to Foster Care.* Lyme Regis: Russell House Publishing.

Rotherham Safeguarding Children Board (2009) *Executive Summary of the Overview Report of a Serious Case Review in Respect of Child V (Female) and Other Children Placed by Rotherham MBC with Foster Carers Mr and Mrs A.* Rotherham: Rotherham Safeguarding Children Board.

Rotherham Safeguarding Children Board (2010) *Executive Summary of Serious Case Review Mr and Mrs B (Foster Carers).* Rotherham: Rotherham Safeguarding Children Board.

Rule, G (2006) *Recruiting Black and Minority Ethnic Adopters and Foster Carers.* London: BAAF.

Schofield, G (2003) *Part of the Family: Pathways through Foster Care.* London: BAAF.

Schofield, G and Beek, M (2006) *Attachment Handbook for Foster Care and Adoption.* London: BAAF.

Schofield, G and Beek, M (2008) *Achieving Permanence in Foster Care: A Good Practice Guide.* London: BAAF.

Schofield, G and Beek, M (2009) *Providing a Secure Base*. Norwich: The University of East Anglia, www.uea.ac.uk/providingasecurebase/uses-of-the-model/the-assessment-of-prospective-foster-carers-and-adopters

Schofield, G and Simmonds, J (eds) (2009) *The Child Placement Handbook: Research, Policy and Practice*. London: BAAF.

Schofield, G and Ward, E (2011) *Understanding and Working with Parents of Children in Long-Term Foster Care*. London: Jessica Kingsley Publishers.

Schofield, G and Ward, E, with Warman, A, Simmonds, J and Butler, J (2008) *Permanence in Foster Care: A Study of Care Planning and Practice in England and Wales*. London: BAAF.

Schofield, G, Beek, M and Ward, E (2012) Part of the family: planning for permanence in long-term family foster care. *Children and Youth Services Review*, 34: 244–53.

Scott, A and Duncan, C (2013) *Understanding Attitudes, Motivations and Barriers to Adoption and Fostering: A Marketing Proposal for the Department of Education*. London: Kindred/Department of Education.

Sebba, J (2012) *Why Do People Become Foster Carers? An International Literature Review on the Motivation to Foster*. Oxford: Rees Centre, Oxford University.

Sellick, C (2006) From famine to feast: a review of the foster care research literature. *Children and Society*, 20: 109–22.

Sellick, C (2011) Towards a mixed economy of foster care provision, in Harlow, E (ed) *Foster Care Matters*. London: Whiting and Birch Ltd.

Sellick, C and Thoburn, J (1996) *What Works in Family Placement?* Barkingside: Barnardo's.

Sellick, C, Thoburn, J and Philpot, T (2004) *What Works in Adoption and Foster Care?* Barkingside: Barnardo's.

Simmonds, J (2011) *The Role of Special Guardianship: Best Practice in Permanency Planning for Children (England and Wales)*. London: BAAF.

Simmonds, J (2013) *Fostering for Adoption: Practice Guidance*. London: Coram Centre for Early Permanence/BAAF.

Sinclair, I (2005) *Fostering Now: Messages from Research*. London: Jessica Kingsley Publishers.

Sinclair, I, Baker, C, Lee, J and Gibbs, I (2007) *The Pursuit of Permanence: A Study of the English Child Care System*. London: Jessica Kingsley Publishers.

Slade, J (2012) *Safer Caring: A New Approach*. London: The Fostering Network.

Smale, G and Tuson, G, with Biehal, N and Marsh, P (1993) *Empowerment, Assessment, Care Management and the Skilled Worker*. London: NISW/HMSO.

Smith, C (2011) Foster care in transition: from waiting in the wings to centre stage, in Harlow, E (ed) *Foster Care Matters*. London: Whiting and Birch Ltd.

Social Care Institute for Excellence (2004) *SCIE Guide 7: Fostering*. London: SCIE, www.scie.org.uk/publications/guides/guide07/files/guide07.pdf

Talbot, C and Wheal, A (2005) Education and training for foster carers and social workers, in Wheal, A (ed) *The RHP Companion to Foster Care*. Lyme Regis: Russell House Publishing.

Tapsfield, R (2013) *Foster Care Fortnight: Thank You*. London: The Fostering Network, www.fostering.net/news/2013/foster-care-fortnight-thank-you#.UaeEiCRwaM9

The College of Social Work (2012) *Mapping of the PCF against the SoPs: June 2012*. London: College of Social Work.

The Fostering Network (2004) *Good Practice Guidelines for the Recruitment of Foster Carers*. London: The Fostering Network.

The Fostering Network (2009) *The Skills to Foster*. London: The Fostering Network.

The Fostering Network (2010a) *The Skills to Foster Assessment. Applying to Foster: An Applicant's Guide to the Assessment Process*. London: The Fostering Network.

The Fostering Network (2010b) *The Skills to Foster Assessment. Assessing Foster Carers: A Social Worker's Guide*. London: The Fostering Network.

The Fostering Network (2013) *Foster Carer Recruitment to Reach Next Level with New Government Contract*. London: The Fostering Network, www.fostering.net/news/2013/foster-carer-recruitment-reach-next-level-new-government-contract#.UaeFHiRwaM8

The Scottish Executive (2005) *National Care Standards Foster Care and Family Placement Services*. Edinburgh: Scottish Executive.

The Scottish Executive and the Fostering Network (2004) *Code of Practice on the Recruitment, Assessment, Approval, Training, Management and Support of Foster Carers in Scotland*. London: The Fostering Network.

Thomas, N (2009) Listening to children and young people, in Schofield, G and Simmonds, J (eds) *The Child Placement Handbook: Research, Policy and Practice*. London: BAAF, pp63–80.

Thomas, M and Philpot, T (2009) *Fostering a Child's Recovery: Family Placement for Traumatised Children*. London: Jessica Kingsley Publishers.

Triseliotis, J, Borland, M and Hill, M (2000) *Delivering Foster Care*. London: BAAF.

UK Joint Working Party on Foster Care (1999a) *UK National Standards for Foster Care*. London: National Foster Care Association.

UK Joint Working Party on Foster Care (1999b) *Code of Practice on the Recruitment, Assessment, Approval, Training, Management and Support of Foster Carers*. London: National Foster Care Association.

Utting, W (1997) *People Like Us: The Report of the Review of the Safeguards for Children Living Away from Home*. London: HMSO.

Wade, J, Sirriyeh, A, Kohli, R and Simmonds, J (2012) *Fostering Unaccompanied Asylum-Seeking Young People: Creating a Family Life Across a 'World of Difference'*. London: BAAF.

Wales Code of Practice Working Group (1999) *Code of Practice, Wales: Recruitment, Assessment, Approval, Training, Management and Support of Foster Carers*. London: National Foster Care Association.

Walker, S and Beckett, C (2010) *Social Work Assessment and Intervention* (2nd edition). Lyme Regis: Russell House Publishing.

Warman, A, Pallett, C and Scott, S (2006) Learning from each other: process and outcomes in the fostering changes training programme. *Adoption and Fostering*, 30(3): 17–28.

Welsh Assembly Government (2003) *National Minimum Standards for Fostering Services*. Cardiff: Welsh Assembly Government.

Wheal, A and Mehmet, M (2012) *The Foster Carer's Handbook for Carers of Children 11 Years and Under*. Lyme Regis: Russell House Publishing.

Whittington, C (2007) *Assessment in Social Work: A Guide for Learning and Teaching*. London: Social Care Institute for Excellence.

Wilson, K and Sinclair, I (2004) Contact in foster care: some dilemmas and opportunities, in Neil, E and Howe, D (eds) *Contact in Adoption and Permanent Foster Care: Research, Theory and Practice*. London: BAAF, pp165–83.

Wilson, K, Sinclair, I, Taylor, C, Pithouse, A and Sellick, C (2004) *Fostering Success: An Exploration of the Research Literature in Foster Care. Knowledge Review 5*. London: Social Care Institute for Excellence/ Bristol: Policy Press.

Wilson, K, Ruch, G, Lymbery, M and Cooper, A (2011) *Social Work: An Introduction to Contemporary Practice* (2nd edition). Harlow: Pearson/Longman.

Wonnacot, J (2012) *Mastering Social Work Supervision*. London: Jessica Kingsley Publishers.

Index